Jane Asher's
EATS ◆ FOR ◆ TREATS

OVER 40 DELICIOUS RECIPES TO COOK WITH YOUR CHILD

BBC BOOKS

For Sarah and Helen, with love from Aunt Jane

Photographed by: Jerry Tubby
Food prepared by Berit Vinegrad

The Cuisinox saucepans used for testing were supplied by ICTC

Published by BBC Books
A division of BBC Enterprises Limited
Woodlands, 80 Wood Lane
London W12 0TT

First published 1990
© Myriad Productions Limited 1990

ISBN 0 563 36004 6

Colour origination by Imago Publishing Ltd
Photosetting by Goodfellow & Egan Ltd, Cambridge
Cover printed in Great Britain by Belmont Press, Northampton
Text printed and bound in Great Britain by Butler & Tanner Ltd,
Frome and London

CONTENTS

ACKNOWLEDGEMENTS

Writing this book has been enormous fun — especially so due to the enthusiastic support and inspiration of my two friends and colleagues at the BBC: Suzanne Webber and Mary Clyne, without whom the book would not exist.

Many thanks also to the indispensable Vicky Kimm, Martha Caute, Frank Phillips and Wendy Hobson. Much appreciation to Mark Lucas and Kirsty Ackland for their constant encouragement.

Sandra Yong and I spent many happy hours together cooking and tasting recipes, and Berit Vinegrad and Emma-Lee Gow made them look stunning for the pictures.

I was very lucky to have Jerry Tubby and his assistant Simon Whitmore to take such wonderful photographs, and Ann Salisbury to design the book so beautifully.

As usual I am very grateful to my family — Gerald, Katie, Alexander and Rory — for putting up with the chaos of recipe testing and writing, and especially for being willing guinea-pigs when it came to tasting.

Charterhouse Square School, London, Karen Copeland and the headmistress Jennifer Mason were extremely helpful, and I must say a very special thank you to the following children from the school who tested the recipes for me. Together with their parents, they not only shopped, cooked and tasted, but took the trouble to give me their constructive and encouraging comments:

Meera Acharya   Katherine Munsey
David Benson   David O'Leary
Alessia Blake   Brijesh Patel
Victoria Brailsford   Rima Patel
Elizabeth Cooksey   Holly Power
Camilla Cope   Douglas Renwick
Olivia Dore   Thristian Richards
Gemma Doughty   Alex Russell
Rebecca Greenslade   Caspar Searle
Sarah Kate Hammond   Laura Singleton-Turner
Suzanne Harmer   Alexander Taylor
Helen Havercroft   Emma Waites
Raphaëlle Heaf   Hedi Young
Alex McHugh

INTRODUCTION

Cooking a meal – or even one dish – for yourself or your family or friends can be one of life's most satisfying experiences. We all need food to survive, but eating has become much more than just a way of keeping our bodies going: sharing a meal is an extremely enjoyable event, and some of my happiest moments are working in the kitchen to prepare one.

I learnt much of my basic cookery from watching my mother; but now that we are offered such a choice of ready meals and convenience foods, there is often less practical cooking in the home. There is nothing wrong with some of the delicious prepared meals that are available – and all of us have dashed out to the supermarket and bought them when we just don't feel like cooking – but it would be a shame if you missed out on the pleasure of preparing something entirely yourself.

It's impossible for me to know how much cookery you have already done. You may find some of the recipes are too easy for you and some too difficult; you will have to find your own level and work from there. Also, you must discuss it with a grown-up when you decide to cook; depending on your age and skill you may need help with everything, or just someone keeping an eye. Cooking involves heat and knives – both potentially dangerous – and I don't want any of you to take any risks. I have put symbols in the recipes to remind you when you must have an adult watching: ✎ for knives, ◍ for heat.

When you start these recipes, I suggest you follow the instructions exactly; even a slight change of quantities can ruin the result. As you become more experienced, you may want to start varying things a little – adding your own favourite ingredient or using a different herb or vegetable. Once you know the basic principles of cookery you may eventually be inventing your own recipes – I'd love to hear from you if you do.

Magic things happen when you cook: ingredients change colour, texture and shape when they are heated; the combination of one food with another can dramatically alter the flavour of both of them; sauces thicken; dough rises; sugar caramelises. The first time you experience one of these miracles is very exciting, and I shall feel proud if I can inspire you to have a go. I just wish I could be there when you start cooking and share your enjoyment, but at least I feel I shall be looking over your shoulder through the pages of this book.

SAFETY HINTS

Cooking is great fun if you are sensible and follow a few simple safety rules. So do be careful, and enjoy your cooking.

1 Tell a grown-up before you start – you may need some help.

2 Be careful with knives, graters, peelers, blenders, processors – anything which has a sharp point or blade. Never cut towards your fingers, keep your fingers behind the cutting blade and use a chopping board.

3 Wear oven gloves when putting anything into or taking anything out of the oven in case you touch the oven by mistake.

4 Any pan or tin which has been in the oven or over heat will be very hot, so do take care. Do not leave hot tins where someone else might touch them.

5 Turn pan handles to the side when cooking so you do not knock into them.

6 Water and electricity do not mix. If you are using electric mixers etc., make sure your hands are dry before you plug in the appliance.

7 Hot liquid is dangerous, so is steam. Never reach across a pan of hot food.

8 Never carry hot pans across the kitchen, you might stumble or bump into someone.

9 Put down hot pans on a heatproof work surface, never on a cold surface, such as tiles, which might crack.

10 Take care when testing or tasting hot food. Sugary foods in particular get very hot indeed.

11 When adding ingredients to hot oil or liquid, do not splash the liquid. Be careful – hot oil may spit.

12 Remember to turn off the oven, grill or burner when you have finished.

13 If you have little brothers or sisters don't let them near the oven or hob. Keep knives out of reach.

14 The recipes are marked with two safety symbols.
means that part of the recipe needs knives or sharp blades.

means that part of the recipe involves cooking.

NOTES ON THE RECIPES

1 The recipes use size 2 eggs, unless I mention a different size in the list of ingredients. If you don't have the right size, use what you have and add a little more or less liquid as necessary.

2 Spoon measurements are level. Fill the spoon with the ingredient you are measuring, then level the top with a knife. It's worth buying a set of plastic measuring spoons – they're very useful and more accurate than any assorted spoons you may find at the bottom of the kitchen drawer.

3 Before you start, get out everything you will need, then measure out or prepare all the ingredients before you begin to cook. As you get more experienced you'll find you don't always bother to do this and will guess measurements and throw things together as you go along, but it's important to start with good habits: you need to learn which ingredients *do* need to be exactly measured.

4 Don't mix metric and imperial measurements, just follow one set.

5 Look at the Basic Techniques at the back of the book if you need extra information.

6 Some people are worried about using raw egg white. Ask a grown-up's advice, and if necessary use dried egg white instead. Just follow the instructions on the packet and add to the recipe.

7 Always wash your hands before you start and after handling raw meat or poultry.

8 Chicken and pork dishes must always be thoroughly cooked.

MINI-FLORENTINES

Makes about 12   Medium easy

a little oil for greasing

50 g (2 oz) glacé cherries

50 g (2 oz) flaked almonds

40 g (1½ oz) butter or hard margarine

50 g (2 oz) caster sugar

2 tablespoons double cream

25 g (1 oz) chopped mixed candied peel

100 g (4 oz) dark chocolate

4 Put the butter and sugar into a small saucepan and stir over a low heat until the sugar is dissolved. Mix in the cream and turn up the heat a little to make it boil (when the top of the mixture bubbles) for 1 minute. Take the saucepan off the heat (remember to turn off the heat), put it on a heatproof surface and stir in the chopped cherries and almonds and the mixed peel. The pan will stay hot, so be careful.

Traditionally florentines are baked in spoonfuls on a baking sheet, but I find it's almost impossible to stop them spreading into each other. This way of cooking them in bun tins is much easier; they look lovely once they're spread with the chocolate. If you want to make larger ones you can get baking tins with larger moulds in them.

1 Turn the oven to 180°C (350°F), gas mark 4.

2 Brush a bun tin with a little oil.

3 Chop up the cherries into little bits, and chop the almond flakes so they're a bit smaller – mind the knife doesn't slip when you're cutting the almonds.

5 Put a teaspoonful of the mixture into each mould in the bun tin. Carefully put the tin in the oven, wearing oven gloves in case you touch part of the oven. Bake for about 10 minutes.

6 Wearing oven gloves, carefully take the tin out of the oven and put it on a heatproof surface where no one will touch it. After about 1 minute, when the florentines have cooled slightly, press down round the edge of each one with a spoon that you keep damping with a little cold water. This neatens them up and makes them easier to get out of the tin.

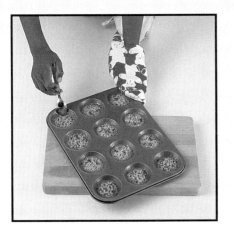

7 Let them cool a little more, then ease them out of the tin with a knife – you can use an ordinary table knife, it needn't be sharp. Put them on a wire rack to get completely cold.

8 Have a grown-up nearby for this. Fill a small saucepan about one-third full of water. Put it on the heat and bring to the boil (bubbling) then turn down the heat so it keeps very hot. Break up the chocolate and put it in a small bowl that will fit into the top of the pan. Stir the chocolate until it melts. You can also melt chocolate very well and easily in a microwave, on full power for about 1 minute.

9 Take the saucepan off the heat (remember to turn it off). With a knife, carefully spread a little hot chocolate on the bottom of each florentine, dipping the knife in hot water between spreadings. Put them upside down until the chocolate is cold and hard, then keep them in an airtight tin.

ALL-IN-ONE SPONGE CAKE

To make one quantity   Medium easy

Makes 1 × 20-cm (8-in) cake; 2 × 18-cm (7-in) cakes; 1 × 18-cm (7-in) square cake

a little oil or margarine for greasing

100 g (4 oz) self-raising flour

1 teaspoon baking powder

100 g (4 oz) soft tub margarine

100 g (4 oz) caster sugar

2 eggs (size 3)

a few drops of vanilla essence

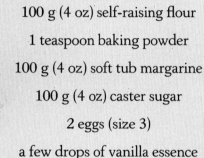

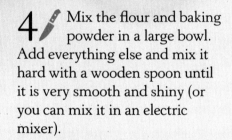

4 Mix the flour and baking powder in a large bowl. Add everything else and mix it hard with a wooden spoon until it is very smooth and shiny (or you can mix it in an electric mixer).

This is a very easy way of making a cake – using the soft margarine and the baking powder means you can mix it all together at once. A cake is a lovely centrepiece for tea, and you can bake it in all sorts of different shapes and decorate it as you like.

1 Turn on the oven to 160°C (325°F), gas mark 3.

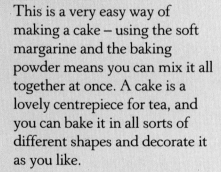

2 Brush the cake tin with oil or rub it with a little margarine.

3 Put the tin on top of a piece of baking parchment and draw round it. Cut out the circle and put it in the bottom of the tin. Grease or oil the paper a little.

5 Spoon it into the tin and smooth the top with the back of a spoon.

6 🔥 Bake in the oven for 35 to 40 minutes for 1 × 20-cm (8-in) cake;
25 to 30 minutes for 2 × 18-cm (7-in) cakes;
35 to 40 minutes for 1 × 18-cm (7-in) square cake.
You must test the cake after the shorter time. Wearing oven gloves, carefully take it out of the oven and press the middle of the cake with your finger. It should feel springy. If it feels soft and a bit soggy put it back for 5 more minutes.

7 🔪🔥 Run a knife round the sides of the tin to make sure it's not stuck anywhere. Put a wire rack on top, then turn the whole thing upside down, holding the tin with your oven gloves as it will still be hot. Take the tin off the cake and peel away the paper. Turn the cake the right way up and leave it to cool completely.

VARIATIONS

1

Chocolate Cake
Only use 75 g (3 oz) of flour, and add 25 g (1 oz) cocoa powder.

2

Coffee Cake
Add 2 teaspoons powdered instant coffee or Camp coffee to the mixture.

3

Coffee Walnut Cake
Add 100 g (4 oz) chopped walnuts to the coffee cake mixture.

4

Lemon or Orange Cake
🔪 Grate the rind of an orange or lemon on the fine side of the grater (mind your fingers). Add it to the mixture.

MADELEINES

Makes about 10   Easy

a little oil or margarine for greasing

1 quantity all-in-one sponge cake mixture
(see page 12) but without the baking powder

4 tablespoons raspberry or strawberry jam

50 g (2 oz) desiccated coconut

5 glacé cherries

a little angelica

Here are some ways of making your sponge cakes look special. These madeleines should really be baked in some little tins called dariole moulds, but if you haven't got any, don't worry – cook them in paper cases, then take off the paper when they are cooked and cooled, before painting them with jam.

1 Turn on the oven to 180°C (350°F), gas mark 4. Brush 10 dariole moulds with oil or grease them with a little margarine (or use paper cases).

2 Fill the dariole moulds or paper cases about three-quarters full of the sponge mixture.

3 Bake in the oven (careful as you put them in) for 15 to 20 minutes until they feel firm on top when you press them with your finger.

4 Wearing oven gloves, take them out of the oven and run a knife around the sides of the moulds. Turn them out of the moulds on to a rack to cool. (If they're in paper cases just leave them to cool.) If possible, leave them overnight before decorating, as they will be easier to handle.

5 Trim off the bottoms (or remove the paper cases) and make sure they are all about the same height.

6 Put the jam in a small saucepan and heat gently to make it runnier, then put through a sieve into a bowl. Be careful – hot jam is *very* hot.

VARIATIONS

7 Push a skewer into each cake to hold it – if it's too soft you may have to hold it gently in your fingers – and brush the bottom and sides with jam. Put the coconut in a saucer and roll each cake in it until it is covered. Put the cakes bottom side up on a plate.

8 Cut the glacé cherries in half, cut leaves out of the angelica and decorate the tops (what were the bottoms) of the madeleines.

1

Fairy Cakes

You can easily make delicious fairy cakes if you stir 50 g (2 oz) of one of these into 1 quantity of all-in-one sponge cake mixture without baking powder: currants, sultanas, raisins, chopped dates, chopped nuts, chopped cherries or chocolate chips. Bake them in paper cases for 15 to 20 minutes and let them get cold. Decorate with cherries and glacé icing (see page 95).

2

Butterfly Cakes

Bake plain fairy cakes and let them get cold. Make 1 quantity of butter icing (see page 95). Peel off the paper cases and slice the tops off the cakes (mind your fingers). Cut each top in two to make two half moons. Spread a little butter icing on each cake and push the two half moons like wings into the icing.

3

Face Cakes

If you ice some fairy cakes with pink glacé icing (see page 95) you can make all sorts of animal and human faces by decorating them with sweets, strips of angelica, glacé cherries, silver balls and so on. Experiment and have fun!

FRIENDS' CAKE

Makes 8 slices   Medium easy

1 quantity all-in-one sponge cake mixture baked in 2 × 18-cm
(7-in) sandwich tins (see page 12)

225 g (8 oz) butter icing (see page 95)

icing sugar for dusting

2 × 250-g (9-oz) packets ready-to-roll fondant icing

food colours

I very much enjoy decorating cakes – if you're doing one for a special celebration it's fun to give the cake a personal touch; it seems a shame to spend hours working hard on a cake which ends up looking as if you bought it from a shop. The traditional way is to use either butter icing

or royal icing spread over the cake and then to decorate it with piping, but you might enjoy experimenting with fondant icing instead. It's quicker and easier and just like using play dough. I've made a cake here with a slice for each person decorated with their initials.

1 When the cakes are completely cool, spread one half with about two-thirds of the butter icing. Sandwich the cakes together.

2 Spread the rest of the butter icing thinly over the whole of the cake.

3 Dust the work surface and a rolling pin with a little icing sugar (so the fondant icing won't stick). Open one packet of icing and knead it with your hands to soften it. You may need a

grown-up to help do this, as it must be soft enough to roll out. Roll it out until it is large enough to cover the cake.

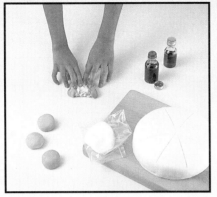

4 Lift the sheet of icing over the cake and smooth round the sides with your hands until it is stuck all over. Trim any extra icing away from the bottom.

5 Mark the cake into 8 slices with the knife, but not cutting right through the icing.

6 Open the other packet of icing. Knead it very well as before until it's soft. Keeping the rest in a plastic bag, colour little pieces of icing one at a time by kneading in drops of food colouring. Roll out the icing and use cutters or a knife to make shapes or numbers for each slice

of cake. Or make little models – just as you would with plasticine, sticking the bits together with a little water.

7 Stick the cut-outs or models on to the cake by damping them with a little water, or with little pieces of icing.

VARIATIONS

1 If you don't like butter icing you can stick the icing on to the cake with jam.

2 You can finish a sponge cake very simply by filling it with jam or fresh cream and dusting the top with icing sugar.

3 Pour 225 g (8 oz) glacé icing (see page 95) over the top of the cake. Decorate with glacé cherries, angelica, chocolate vermicelli or whatever you like.

BROWNIES

Makes 16   Easy

a little oil or butter for greasing

200 g (7 oz) granulated sugar

3 eggs (or 2 eggs, size 1)

5 tablespoons sunflower or vegetable oil

1 teaspoon vanilla essence

100 g (4 oz) plain flour

¼ teaspoon baking powder

a pinch of salt

25 g (1 oz) cocoa powder

25 g (1 oz) drinking chocolate

100 g (4 oz) walnut pieces

Really chocolatey, gooey brownies are delicious. You can spread them with a topping (see Variations) or even serve them warm with cream or ice-cream. It's important that you use exactly the ingredients and method I have described – the sugar must be granulated, for instance, to give the right texture and make the crust on the top, and you must let the brownies cool in the tin. It's better to slightly undercook them rather than leave them in the oven too long, so they have that lovely chewiness. You can leave out the walnuts if you don't like them.

1 Turn on the oven to 180°C (350°F), gas mark 4. Grease and line the base of a 20-cm (8-in) square baking tin. (See All-in-One Sponge Cake, page 12, step 3.)

2 Put the sugar, eggs, oil and vanilla essence into a medium-sized bowl and mix them together. Use a wooden spoon and move it as fast as you can until the mixture is smooth (this is called beating).

3 Put a sieve over another medium-sized bowl and put the flour, baking powder, salt, cocoa and drinking chocolate into it. Push them through the sieve with a spoon, and mix them well together.

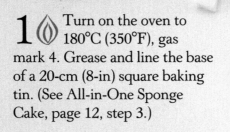

4 Add the flour mixture to the egg mixture and put in the walnuts if you like them. Beat it all together for 1 minute.

5 ◊ Pour the mixture into the baking tin and smooth the top with the back of a spoon. Put the tin into the oven, wearing oven gloves in case you touch the sides or shelves, and bake for 30 to 35 minutes until just firm.

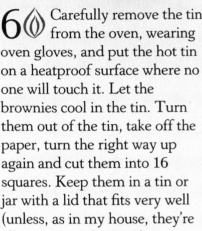

6 ◊ Carefully remove the tin from the oven, wearing oven gloves, and put the hot tin on a heatproof surface where no one will touch it. Let the brownies cool in the tin. Turn them out of the tin, take off the paper, turn the right way up again and cut them into 16 squares. Keep them in a tin or jar with a lid that fits very well (unless, as in my house, they're all eaten straight away).

— VARIATIONS —

1

Really Chocolatey Brownies
Use 50 g (2 oz) cocoa instead of cocoa and drinking chocolate. These are very strong and dark.

2

Chocolate Chip Brownies
Stir 100 g (4 oz) plain, milk or white chocolate drops into the mixture instead of the walnuts.

3

Quick Fudge Topping
◊ Ask a grown-up to help. Put 225 g (8 oz) soft brown sugar, 5 tablespoons double cream, 25 g (1 oz) butter and a pinch of salt into a saucepan. Dissolve everything over a low heat, stirring, then turn up the heat and boil. Take the pan off the heat and let it cool a little. Stir in a few drops of vanilla essence, then beat well until thick. Spread over the cold uncut brownies.

CUT-OUT BISCUITS

Makes about 20   Medium easy

a little oil or butter for greasing

150 g (5 oz) self-raising flour

75 g (3 oz) butter

50 g (2 oz) caster sugar

1 egg (size 3)

a few drops of vanilla essence

Your friends will be really impressed if you give them home-made biscuits when they come round to tea. I've given you two ways of cutting the shapes – either by rolling out and using a cutter, or by making a long roll of dough and slicing it once it's chilled. Don't worry if you haven't got a cutter – a tumbler will do very well. The chilling and slicing way can be useful if you want to keep some dough ready-made in the fridge so you can bake some biscuits at short notice.

1 ⬦ Turn on the oven to 180°C (350°F), gas mark 4. Brush two baking sheets with oil, or grease them with butter.

2 Put the flour in a medium-sized bowl (don't bother to sieve it – flour doesn't have lumps nowadays). Cut the butter into the flour in small pieces.

With both hands scoop up handfuls of butter and flour and rub them between your thumbs and fingers so the pieces of butter get mixed into the flour in smaller and smaller pieces. Keep going until most of the lumps have gone and it looks like breadcrumbs (this is called rubbing in).

3 Add the sugar and mix it in with a wooden spoon. Break the egg into a cup and mix it up well with a fork. Measure 2 tablespoons of egg into the flour mixture and add the vanilla essence. If you've any egg left over, cover it and put it in the fridge – it might be useful for glazing something.

4 Mix the egg and flour mixture together with a fork. Don't worry – it may look as if it will never join together. Keep going, using your hands if it's easier.

5 Sprinkle some flour on your work surface and turn the dough on to it. Squash it with your hands until it is smooth (this is called kneading).

6 Wrap the dough in cling film and put it in the fridge for 30 minutes. Take it out and sprinkle some more flour on the work surface and on to a rolling pin. Roll out the dough to about

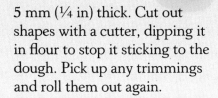

5 mm (¼ in) thick. Cut out shapes with a cutter, dipping it in flour to stop it sticking to the dough. Pick up any trimmings and roll them out again.

7 Put the biscuits on the baking sheet and put them in the oven for about 15 minutes – don't touch any part of the hot oven. Carefully, with oven gloves, take them out and put the sheets down somewhere safe to cool a little, then lift off the biscuits and leave them to cool on a wire rack.

VARIATIONS

1

Refrigerator Cookies
After step 5, shape the dough into a long tube about 15 cm (2 in) across. Wrap it in cling film and chill it for at least 3 hours. Cut it carefully into 5-mm (¼-in) slices then bake the same way as the rolled ones.

2

Any of these biscuits would be delicious and pretty with some glacé icing and decorations on them (see page 95).

3

Orange or Lemon Cookies
Leave out the vanilla essence. Grate the rind of an orange or lemon on the fine side of a grater (mind your fingers). Mix it into the flour before you add the butter.

4

Ginger or Cinnamon Cookies
Leave out the vanilla essence. Add 1 teaspoon ginger powder or cinnamon to the flour.

5

Chocolate Cookies
Only use 100 g (4 oz) flour, and add 25 g (1 oz) cocoa powder instead.

6

Spicy Biscuits
Leave out the vanilla. Crush 1 teaspoon cardamom pods and take out the seeds. Grind the seeds into a powder between two spoons and add them to the flour. Add 2 teaspoons brandy with the egg. These make wonderful Christmas biscuits, and if you cut little holes in each one before you bake them you can thread them with ribbon.

BANANA CAKE

Makes 1 loaf tin cake   Easy

a little oil for greasing

1 egg (size 1)

75 g (3 oz) soft margarine

100 g (4 oz) caster sugar

225 g (8 oz) plain flour

2 teaspoons baking powder

1 orange

1 lemon

4 medium-sized bananas

3 Break the egg into a large mixing bowl and mix it up hard with a fork. Add the soft margarine, the sugar, the flour and the baking powder. Mix it all together very well with the fork – this is quite hard work, and if you have an electric mixer it is much easier and quicker. Keep going until it is all really well blended together. Don't worry; it'll look quite dry.

This delicious banana cake is one of my favourites. It actually gets better if you keep it for a day or so, but it smells so wonderful as you take it out of the oven that I always find it gets eaten straight away. It is especially good spread with butter and my favourite is the walnut variation.

1 Turn on the oven to 180°C (350°F), gas mark 4.

2 Brush a loaf tin 8.5 cm × 19 cm (3½ in × 7½ in) with oil. Cut a piece of non-stick baking parchment the size of the bottom by putting the tin on top of the paper and drawing round it before cutting. Put the paper in the tin and brush that with oil too.

4 Very carefully grate the rind off the orange and the lemon and add the rind to the mixture.

5 Peel the bananas, then put them into a small bowl and mash them up very well with a fork.

6 Add the bananas to the other mixture and mix it all together very well – again using the electric mixer if you have one.

7 Put the mixture into the loaf tin and smooth down the top with a spoon.

8 Put the tin carefully in the oven – wear oven gloves in case you touch the sides of the oven – and let it bake for 50 to 55 minutes. It should feel good and springy on the top when you press it with your finger, but be careful as the tin will be very hot.

9 Let the cake cool in the tin for 10 minutes or so, then turn it out on to a rack to finish getting cold.

VARIATIONS

1

Banana and Walnut Cake
Add 50 g (2 oz) chopped walnuts when you put in the mashed bananas.

2

Crunchy Topping
When you've put the mixture in the tin, sprinkle the top with 1½ tablespoons demerara sugar.

3

Iced Banana Loaf
When the cake is completely cold spread it with 100 g (4 oz) glacé icing (see page 95) then decorate it with walnuts or glacé cherries.

HOME-MADE BREAD

Makes 2 × 450-g (1-lb) loaves   Easy

750 g (1½ lb) strong white flour

2 teaspoons salt

25 g (1 oz) lard or white cooking fat

1 sachet fast action or easy blend yeast

450 ml (¾ pint) warm water (I'll tell you how to get it the right temperature in the recipe)

a little oil for greasing

It makes you feel really clever when you produce your own bread. *But* – and this is the good part – it's very easy to do. If you use the new fast action or easy blend yeast that you buy in supermarkets it really couldn't be simpler – check the instructions on the packet, some kinds need two 'provings' (see recipe) but the latest type needs only one.

1 Mix the flour and salt in a large bowl.

2 Cut the lard or fat into the flour in little pieces then lift handfuls of the flour and fat and rub it between your fingers and thumbs until all big lumps have gone (this is called rubbing in).

3 Stir in the yeast.

4 Put the kettle on to boil. Put 300 ml (½ pint) of cold water in a measuring jug. Very carefully add boiling water from the kettle until you have 450 ml (¾ pint). This mixture will be just warm to the touch – what they call 'blood heat'.

5 Mix the water into the flour. When it's roughly mixed, sprinkle a little flour on to the work surface and tip the mixture on to it. Now comes the fun: push and pull and fold and bash the mixture until it changes into a lovely springy, elastic dough (this is called kneading). Use all your strength – the harder you work the better the bread. It will take at least 5 minutes, maybe more like 10.

6 Cut or pull the dough in two halves and shape them into loaf shapes. Put them on the baking sheets, cover them with oiled cling film, then put them in a warm place until they are twice as big as they were (they will rise up all on their own – magic!). This is called 'proving' the dough. If the yeast you are using needs two provings, follow the instructions on the packet.

7 Turn on the oven to 230°C (450°F), gas mark 8 and let it get hot (about 20 minutes). Bake the loaves (careful as you put them in) for about 30 minutes until golden on top.

8 Wearing oven gloves, take them out of the oven and turn them over. Tap the underneath – if it sounds hollow the bread is cooked, if not put them back in the oven for a little longer.

9 Put on a wire rack to cool. You should really wait until they're cold before cutting them, but if you can't resist it, eat a little piece while it's warm – it tastes wonderful.

VARIATIONS

1

You can use wholemeal flour instead of white and of course you can make the loaves any shape you like or cook them in oiled loaf tins to look professional. Try dividing the dough in three and plaiting it. Make your loaves golden and shiny by brushing them with beaten egg before baking.

2

For a pizza, make half the basic bread mixture. Let it rise in a big bowl in a warm place, then squash it down and knead it a little more. Press it into an ungreased shallow baking tin about 25 × 28 cm (10 × 11 in), and make a raised edge all round. Brush it with oil then put on tomato purée, sliced Mozarella, sliced tomato and whatever else you like. Let it sit for about 15 minutes before baking it at 220°C (425°F), gas mark 7 for about 20 minutes.

PEPPERMINT CREAMS

Makes about 60 to 70   Easy   No cook

1 egg (size 3)

2 tablespoons double cream

480 g (17 oz) icing sugar, sieved to remove lumps

2 teaspoons peppermint essence

a few drops of green food colouring

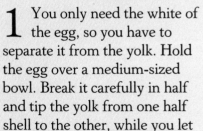

All these sweets on this page and the next are easy to make and look and taste wonderful. Don't eat them too often or you'll ruin your teeth; keep them for special treats or make them for presents packed in little boxes.

1 You only need the white of the egg, so you have to separate it from the yolk. Hold the egg over a medium-sized bowl. Break it carefully in half and tip the yolk from one half shell to the other, while you let the white drop into the bowl. You may need a grown-up to help, as you mustn't let any yolk get in at all, or you may prefer to use a substitute (see page 9). Whisk up the white with a fork until it's frothy. Stir in the cream.

2 Bit by bit, stir the icing sugar into the egg white and cream with a wooden spoon. Keep stirring until it is smooth. If it is too runny to knead with your fingers, add a little more icing sugar.

1

Coffee Creams
Instead of the peppermint essence use coffee essence, and add a little brown colouring if you like.

2

You can make almost any flavour in the same way, using strawberry, orange, lemon essences and so on.

3

Chocolate Creams
Dip half of each peppermint cream in melted chocolate.

3 Add the peppermint essence drop by drop, mixing it in with your hands and tasting as you go to get it as strong as you like.

4 Divide the mixture in half. Colour one half green by kneading in a few drops of colouring.

5 Dust a board or work surface and a rolling pin with icing sugar. Roll out the mixture about 5 mm (¼ in) thick. Cut into shapes, picking up the trimmings and rolling them again until it is all used.

6 Put them on to non-stick paper to dry overnight or for at least 12 hours, then keep them in a tin with a well fitting lid.

CHOCOLATE TRUFFLES

Makes 24   Easy   No cook except for melting chocolate

225 g (8 oz) good plain chocolate

25 g (1 oz) butter

1 tablespoon cream or evaporated milk

1 teaspoon vanilla essence

2 tablespoons cocoa powder

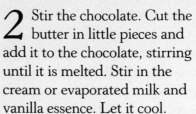

As well as making a lovely present, sweets can be served at the end of a meal to finish it off in a very special way. Put them into little paper cases and on to a smart plate – you might even be able to buy a pretty paper doyley to put under them.

1 Break the chocolate into a medium-sized heatproof bowl. To melt the chocolate, fit the bowl over a saucepan of very hot water. You can do this off the heat for safety, but it will take a little time.

2 Stir the chocolate. Cut the butter in little pieces and add it to the chocolate, stirring until it is melted. Stir in the cream or evaporated milk and vanilla essence. Let it cool.

3 Put it in the fridge for about 30 minutes until it is stiff enough to handle. Take small spoonfuls and roll them between your hands into balls. Put the cocoa in a small dish and roll the truffles in it until they are covered.

VARIATIONS

1

You can roll the truffles in icing sugar, chocolate strands or chocolate flakes for a change.

2

Rum or Brandy and Raisin Truffles
Instead of the vanilla essence use 2 teaspoons rum or brandy flavouring (or real rum or brandy if you're making them for a grown-up). Stir in 75 g (3 oz) raisins at the same time.

3

Marzipan Truffles
Chop 75 g (3 oz) marzipan into tiny pieces. Stir it into the truffle mixture before cooling.

4

Marzipan Shapes
You can buy ready-made marzipan; try to get white rather than yellow. Model small pieces of marzipan into fruits: apples, pears, bananas. Let them dry a little then paint them with food colours. Use cloves for stalks. Take the stones out of some dates and fill the insides with marzipan; roll the dates in caster sugar and put them in paper cases. Colour small pieces of marzipan by kneading in some food colour, roll them into little balls then press a nut into the top of each. Colour ¼ packet marzipan pink and ¼ packet green. Dust the work surface with icing sugar and roll out the marzipan into rectangles. Damp the top of one piece and stick the other on top, then roll them up together, starting from the long side. Cut into thin slices to make pretty spirals.

AMERICAN MUFFINS

Makes 10 to 12 muffins   Easy

a little oil for greasing

225 g (8 oz) plain flour

100 g (4 oz) caster sugar

2 teaspoons baking powder

½ teaspoon salt

1 egg (size 1)

250 ml (8 fl oz) milk

120 ml (4 fl oz) sunflower or vegetable oil

I was very confused when I first went to America and was offered an 'English Muffin'. It was unlike anything I had ever eaten, and quite delicious; I suppose they were popular in England in the olden days (there's a famous song, 'Can You Hear the Muffin Man?') but went out of fashion. But American muffins are rather different – more like a cake than a bread, and often served warm for breakfast. I love them.

1 Turn on the oven to 200°C (400°F), gas mark 6.

2 Stand double paper cases inside each dip in a bun tin, or use oiled muffin tins.

3 Mix the flour, sugar, baking powder and salt in a large bowl.

4 In a different bowl mix the egg, milk and oil very well together with a fork.

5 Make a dip in the middle of the flour mixture and pour in the liquid ingredients. Stir it all together until the dry things are mixed in but it's still all lumpy – this is very important as if you mix it too much the muffins will be tough.

6 ◊ Using a spoon or an ice-cream scoop if you have one, fill the paper cases or muffin tins nearly full (they will rise up when they're cooked). Put them carefully in the oven (remember to wear oven gloves) for about 20 minutes. They should look a little brown and feel springy when you press them gently with your finger.

7 ◊ Wearing oven gloves, take them carefully out of the oven and let them cool.

VARIATIONS

1

Fruit Muffins
Stir in 200 g (7 oz) fresh or tinned and drained blackcurrants, cranberries, blackberries, blueberries, chopped apple or raspberries and ½ teaspoon cinnamon into the dry flour mixture. If you use the tinned fruit it will be a little wet, so only use 175–200 ml (6–7 fl oz) milk.

2

Chocolate Chip Muffins
Use 40 g (1½ oz) cocoa powder and 175 g (6 oz) flour instead of the 225 g (8 oz) flour in the basic recipe. Stir in 100 g (4 oz) plain or milk chocolate chips into the dry flour mixture. Add ½ teaspoon vanilla essence to the egg, oil and milk.

3

Peanut Butter and Banana Muffins
Use wholemeal flour instead of white. Use soft brown sugar instead of caster sugar and add ¼ teaspoon cinnamon and ¼ teaspoon nutmeg to the dry flour mixture. Mash two bananas with 2 tablespoons crunchy peanut butter. Stir the egg, oil and milk into the banana mixture and then stir in the flour etc.

CHOCOLATE BISCUIT CAKE

Makes 1 × 18-cm (7-in) round cake   Easy

a little oil for greasing

2 eggs (size 3)

25 g (1 oz) caster sugar

4 drops of vanilla essence

100 g (4 oz) butter or margarine

225 g (8 oz) plain chocolate

225 g (8 oz) digestive biscuits

a little icing sugar for dusting

1 mint leaf

This is one of the most wicked and delicious treats I know. Only to be eaten very occasionally, and only in tiny slices, as it's very rich and chocolatey. It's often made in a square tin, but I think the round one cut in wedges looks very elegant.

1 Brush an 18-cm (7-in) round cake tin with oil. Cut a circle of non-stick baking parchment to fit the bottom, by putting the tin on the paper and drawing round it before cutting. Put the paper in the tin and brush it with oil.

2 Break the eggs into a medium-sized bowl and add

the sugar and vanilla essence. Mix them very well together with a fork or whisk until they are frothy (this is called beating).

3 Cut the butter into small pieces, place it in a small saucepan and melt it over a gentle heat.

4 Turn up the heat under the butter until it is bubbling then quickly pour it into the egg mixture, stirring all the time – it might be easier to do this with help. Then pour it

back into the saucepan and cook it *over a very gentle heat* until it thickens like thick cream. Don't let it boil or it will separate into lumps and liquid (curdle). When it is thick turn off the heat and put it on one side.

5 Put a saucepan of water on the heat and let it get very hot until it is nearly bubbling (boiling). Break up the chocolate and put it in a small bowl. Fit the bowl on top of the saucepan and let the chocolate melt, stirring it every now and then. Do be careful as hot steam can escape from round the bowl. You can do this off the heat, but it will take longer. If you have a microwave, put the chocolate in a microwaveable bowl in the oven on full power for about 1 to 2 minutes until melted, then stir it well.

6 Pour or spoon the chocolate on to the egg mixture and mix well.

7 Put the biscuits in a clean tea towel or strong plastic bag and bash them with a rolling pin until they're broken up and mostly crushed (but don't bash yourself!).

8 Stir the biscuits into the chocolate mixture and spoon it into the tin. Press down and smooth the top with the back of a wooden spoon. Put it in the fridge for at least 3 hours to set – even better overnight.

9 Turn the cake out of the tin and peel the paper off the bottom. Turn it the right way up again, then sprinkle the top with sieved icing sugar and, if you like, decorate with a mint leaf.

VARIATIONS

1

Add one of these to the mixture:
25 g (1 oz) chopped almonds, walnuts or hazelnuts;
25 g (1 oz) chopped preserved or crystallised ginger.

2

For a really special occasion, add 50 g (2 oz) washed and chopped glacé cherries with the nuts. Melt 175 g (6 oz) chocolate and spread it over the mixture in the tin. When it's almost set, mark the chocolate into the sixteen wedges or you'll find it impossible to cut later. Don't use the icing sugar on top.

FLAPJACKS

Makes 8   Easy

a little oil, butter or margarine for greasing

75 g (3 oz) butter or margarine

75 g (3 oz) soft brown sugar

50 g (2 oz) golden syrup

175 g (6 oz) rolled oats

I think everyone loves flapjacks and they are not at all difficult to make. If you cut them into small pieces and put them in a tin they would make a lovely present, or make the muesli bars and take them to school for break or part of your lunch box.

1 Turn on the oven to 180°C (350°F), gas mark 4. Brush an 18-cm (7-in) square tin with oil, or grease it with a little butter or margarine.

2 Cut the butter in small pieces and put it in a medium saucepan with the sugar and syrup. Being very careful, stir it over a gentle heat until it is all melted.

3 Take the pan off the heat – careful, the handle may be hot – and put it down somewhere heatproof. Turn off the heat. Stir in the rolled oats.

4 Spoon the mixture into the baking tin and smooth it down with the back of the spoon.

5 Put the tin carefully in the oven and bake for 20 minutes or until golden brown.

6 Wearing oven gloves, take the tin out of the oven (don't forget to turn off the oven) and put it somewhere safe to cool for a couple of minutes.

7 Mark it into 8 pieces with a knife. Let it get completely cold then turn it out of the tin and break it into squares. Keep them in a tin with a well fitting lid.

VARIATIONS

1

Muesli Bars
Use muesli instead of oats and cut them into rectangles.

2

Ginger Flapjacks
Add about ½ teaspoon ground ginger to the rolled oats before you stir them into the butter, sugar and syrup.

3

Chocolate Crispies
Add 2 tablespoons of cocoa powder to the melted butter, sugar and syrup off the heat. Let it cool slightly, then add 75 g (3 oz) cornflakes. Mix well, then pile into paper cases and let them get completely cold.

— CHOCOLATE ECLAIRS —

Makes about 18   Advanced

a little oil or butter for greasing

For the pastry:

150 ml (¼ pint) water

50 g (2 oz) butter

65 g (2½ oz) strong flour (or ordinary flour, but strong makes them a better texture)

2 eggs (size 3), well beaten

For the filling:

150 ml (¼ pint) double cream

1 tablespoon icing sugar

For the topping:

75 g (3 oz) icing sugar

2 tablespoons cocoa powder

2 tablespoons very hot water

You use a special kind of pastry to make éclairs. It is called choux pastry, and it's one of the easiest to make as long as you've got a strong arm, as you need to mix it very well and hard for quite a long time. If you can get a friend to make it with you you'll find the extra pair of hands very helpful. It doesn't keep well at all, so anything made with choux really needs to be eaten the same day that you make it, but I don't think you'll find that's a problem . . .

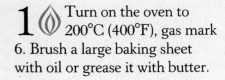

1 Turn on the oven to 200°C (400°F), gas mark 6. Brush a large baking sheet with oil or grease it with butter.

2 Put the water into a medium-sized saucepan. Cut the butter into small pieces and put it in the water. Put the saucepan on to a medium heat and stir the butter and water with a wooden spoon until the butter has melted. As soon as the water begins to bubble, take the pan off the heat (careful, it'll be very hot now) and put it on a heatproof surface. Turn off the heat.

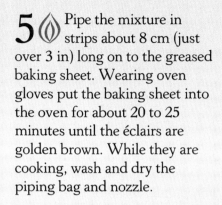

5 Pipe the mixture in strips about 8 cm (just over 3 in) long on to the greased baking sheet. Wearing oven gloves put the baking sheet into the oven for about 20 to 25 minutes until the éclairs are golden brown. While they are cooking, wash and dry the piping bag and nozzle.

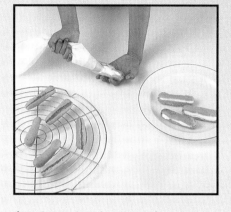

3 Quickly tip all the flour in at once, stirring it at the same time with the wooden spoon (this is the first time your friend would come in very useful). Keep mixing it very hard (take turns if you've got help) until it's smooth, then add the eggs, little by little, beating hard all the time until the mixture is smooth and a bit shiny.

4 To make the proper éclair shape you'll need a large nylon or polythene piping bag, fitted with a plain 1-cm (½-in) piping nozzle. Turn over the top of the bag so it doesn't get sticky, then get your helper to hold it wide open while you spoon in the pastry mixture.

6 Carefully take the éclairs out of the oven (don't forget your oven gloves). Lift them on to a rack to cool, and make a tiny hole in the side of each one to let out the steam.

7 Mix the cream and icing sugar (you needn't bother to sieve it) in a medium-sized bowl, and whisk it very hard with a fork or a whisk until it is thick (see page 94). Put the nozzle in the piping bag then spoon in the cream mixture. Carefully cut each éclair along one side, pipe the cream inside then push the top back gently.

8 Mix the icing sugar and cocoa powder in a small bowl (you needn't sieve it). Add the hot water bit by bit, stirring all the time, until it's soft enough to spread, without getting runny. Spread a little icing on top of each éclair.

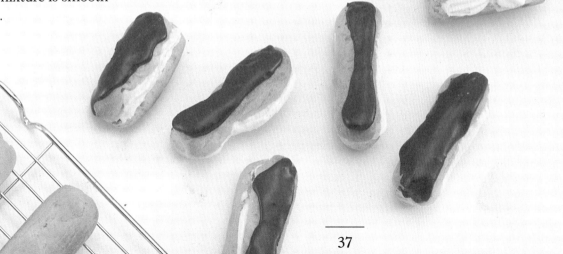

SPANISH OMELETTE

PICNICS AND BARBECUES

Serves 4   Medium easy

1 large Spanish onion

450 g (1 lb) potatoes (ask for 'waxy' ones)

6 tablespoons vegetable or olive oil

4 eggs

salt and black pepper

Making a French omelette can be quite tricky, but this way of cooking one is easier and good for picnics. You can eat it hot or cold, and it's lovely with a crisp green salad.

1 Being very careful of your fingers, take the skin off the onion, cut it in half and slice it thinly. Peel the potatoes and cut them into small dice – about the size of your thumb nail (see page 94).

2 Put half the oil in a large non-stick frying pan and let it get hot over a medium heat for a minute or so. Carefully add the onion and potato, watching that the oil does not splash. Cook for 5 to 10 minutes, stirring every now and then so it doesn't burn. The onion should be golden brown and the potato soft. Taste a piece of potato to make sure it is cooked – but do be careful, it will be very hot. Take the pan off the heat, put it down on something heatproof and turn off the heat.

3 Break the eggs into a bowl – fish out any shell – and beat well with a fork or whisk. Sprinkle with salt and pepper, then stir in the potato and onion. Carefully wipe out with kitchen paper.

VARIATIONS

You could add any of these to the frying pan with the potato and onion.

1

 Cut the tops off 1 small red and 1 small green pepper. Pull out and throw away the seeds and white pith. Cut the peppers into strips then into small dice (see page 94).

2

Cut 100 g (4 oz) streaky bacon or ham into small dice.

3

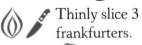 Thinly slice 3 frankfurters.

4 Turn on the grill. Heat the oil in the frying pan over a medium heat and pour in the egg. Turn the heat to low. Cook without stirring for 3 to 5 minutes until just set.

5 Remove the pan and turn off the heat. Place the pan under the grill for 2 to 3 minutes until the top is cooked and golden brown. Tip the omelette out on to a large plate and cut it into wedges.

PASTIES

Makes 4   Medium easy

225 g (8 oz) stewing steak

1 medium potato

1 small onion

a little fresh parsley

salt and pepper

flour for rolling out the pastry

350 g (12 oz) shortcrust pastry (see page 95) or use frozen

25 g (1 oz) butter

milk or beaten egg to glaze

Pasties can be eaten hot or cold, and are very good for carrying around at a picnic without getting sticky fingers. You can use all sorts of different fillings. In the old days, pasties were sometimes made with savoury ingredients one end and sweet the other, so that someone working out in the fields all day would have the first course and pudding all in one pastry parcel.

1 Turn on the oven to 220°C (425°F) gas mark 7. Cut all the gristle and fat off the stewing steak, chop it

into tiny pieces and put it in a medium-sized bowl. You'll need to use a sharp knife for this so be very careful or ask a grown-up to do it. Peel the vegetables and cut them into tiny squares (see page 94) then carefully chop the parsley and add it with the vegetables to the meat. Sprinkle a little salt and pepper on top and mix well.

2 Sprinkle the work surface and your rolling pin with flour (so the pastry doesn't stick to them) and roll out the pastry until it's big enough to make four circles about 20 cm (8 in) across. Cut round a plate or large saucer (*please* be careful – don't let the

40

1

Try using ham, bacon or chicken instead of the stewing steak. Or if you don't like meat, you can easily fill your pasties with your favourite vegetables. Something like: potato, onion and fried mushrooms; potato, onion, carrot and celery; potato, peas and sweetcorn.

2

Sweet Pasties

Peel and core 4 small cooking or eating apples then chop them into small pieces (see page 94). Put a quarter into each pastry circle, add a few sultanas, a squeeze of lemon juice and about a dessert-spoonful of sugar (or less if they are sweet eating apples) before you add the butter. Don't add parsley, salt or pepper. When you turn down the oven, bake them for an extra 30 minutes.

knife slip) to make 4 neat circles of pastry. Put them to one side, gather up the pastry trimmings and roll them out again. Cut out little decorations like leaves or letters (your friends' initials?). Spoon a quarter of the filling on to half of each circle then put little bits of butter on top.

3 Brush the edges of the pastry with a little water and fold the pastry over the filling to give a half-moon shape. Press the edges firmly together then pinch into a wavy pattern with your fingers (this is called crimping).

4 Brush the pasties with milk or with beaten egg if you like them shiny (this is called glazing). Stick the initials or leaves on to each corner, then glaze them as well. Make a little hole in the top of each pasty with your knife (to let the steam out while they are cooking).

5 Place the pasties on baking sheets. Put them into the oven – do wear oven gloves in case you touch the oven by mistake – and bake for 15 minutes, then turn the oven down to 160°C (325°F) gas mark 3 for a further 45 minutes. Wearing oven gloves, carefully remove them from the oven and leave to cool for 5 minutes before eating, or let them get completely cold.

CHICKEN DRUMSTICKS

Serves 4   Easy

4 chicken drumsticks

1 quantity marinade

Everyone loves to eat drumsticks, and you can brush them with oil and bake them just as they are, but if you marinade them first they will be much more interesting. To marinade means to soak something (usually meat) in some sort of liquid before it is cooked. This gives the meat a special taste, and makes it more tender.

1 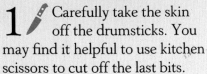 Carefully take the skin off the drumsticks. You may find it helpful to use kitchen scissors to cut off the last bits.

2 With a sharp knife cut the flesh deeply two or three times. This helps the marinade to soak in and also makes the chicken cook right through.

3 Make the marinade and put it in a deep dish. Roll the drumsticks in it, then cover the dish and put it in the fridge. Let the chicken marinade for a few hours – the longer the better.

4 Turn on the oven to 190°C (375°F), gas mark 5. Let it get hot (about 20 minutes).

5 Take the chicken pieces out of the marinade and put them on a rack in a roasting tin. Bake for 30 minutes, but mind you don't touch any part of the oven when you put them in. Wearing oven gloves, carefully brush them with the marinade a couple of times while they are cooking.

MARINADES

1

Orange and Honey
Mix 300 ml (½ pint) orange juice with grated rind of ½ orange, a large pinch of dry mustard and 3 tablespoons each of honey, light soy sauce and lemon juice.

2

Yoghurt, Lemon and Garlic
Mix together 4 tablespoons natural yoghurt, 2 tablespoons lemon juice, the grated rind of ½ lemon, 3 tablespoons oil, 2 skinned and crushed garlic cloves, salt and black pepper.

3

Tandoori
You can buy delicious tandoori paste from the supermarket. Mix 3 tablespoons of the paste with 50 g (2 oz) natural yoghurt. You need only let the chicken marinade for 20 minutes or so.

VARIATION

1

Crispy Drumsticks
If you like crunchy, crispy drumsticks, these are delicious. Crush 2 bags of crisps (smoky bacon flavour works very well) and mix them with 50 g (2 oz) grated cheese. Dip each drumstick into beaten egg then press on the crisp mixture. Bake on an oiled baking tray with any left-over crisps sprinkled on top.

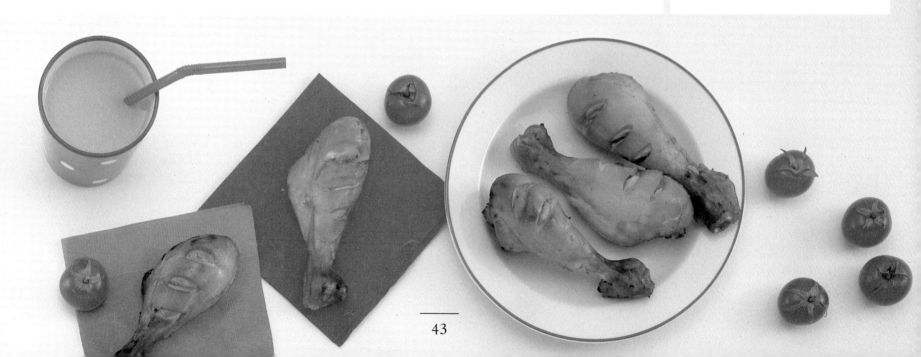

PAN BAGNA

Makes 4 large or 8 small sandwiches   Easy   No cook

1 French stick (or baguette as it's called in French)

olive oil (it must be *olive* oil or it won't taste right)

1 green or red pepper

4 large ripe tomatoes

a few basil leaves, or dried Italian herbs

100 g (4 oz) Mozarella cheese

10 slices salami

salt and black pepper

small tin of anchovy fillets in oil

a few black olives, stones removed

I love sandwiches – they don't have to be boring. You can invent all sorts of different mixtures to fill them: the Americans like peanut butter and jam, for instance, and a young friend of mine is very fond of cream cheese and ketchup. This recipe for Pan Bagna is Italian, very easy to do and quite delicious. You can leave out anything you don't like (I hate peppers) and try it with different things inside. Remember you will need to start the day before so that it can sit in the fridge overnight.

1 Cut the loaf in half lengthways, minding that the knife doesn't slip. Pull out some dough and brush the insides with plenty of oil.

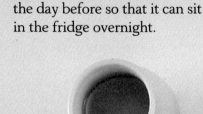

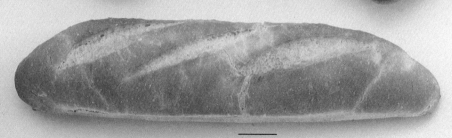

1
After you have wrapped the loaf in foil, instead of chilling it you could bake it in a hot oven at 200°C (400°F), gas mark 6 for about 10 minutes so the cheese melts. Serve hot.

2
Avocado is delicious in sandwiches. Peel one, then cut it in half and take out the stone. Either slice it or mash it up with a fork with a little lemon juice (to stop it going brown). Try it with prawns, lettuce and cream cheese or with grilled chopped bacon.

3
Try bananas in sandwiches, sliced or mixed with honey.

2 Cut the top off the pepper and pull out the seeds and the white pith. Carefully cut the pepper and the tomatoes into thin slices using a very sharp serrated (saw-edged) knife. Cut up the basil leaves a little and slice the Mozarella.

3 Spread out the pieces of salami along the bottom half of the loaf, then make a layer of tomatoes, basil or dried herbs, pepper and cheese.

4 Sprinkle with salt and pepper. Carefully open the tin of anchovies and drain off the oil. Put the anchovies and olives on top of the cheese.

5 Put the other half back on top of the loaf, then wrap it tightly in kitchen foil. Put it in the fridge overnight with a baking sheet on top with a weight on it so it squashes it down a bit.

6 Unwrap the loaf and cut it into 4 large or 8 small sandwiches.

HAMBURGERS

Makes 4 quarter-pounders   Easy

450 g (1 lb) best beef steak

salt and black pepper

4 burger buns

oil for grilling

slices of onion for garnishing

The best American hamburgers are made from top quality meat – rump or sirloin – just minced up and grilled with a little salt and pepper. This of course makes them very expensive, so they can also be made with ordinary best lean mince with a little onion and breadcrumb added; this makes them more like a beefburger, but they're still very tasty, especially if you serve them with a barbecue sauce.

1 Either get your butcher to mince the steak for you or mince it at home in a mincer or food processor.

2 Turn on the grill to high to get hot. Turn on the oven to 150°C (300°F), gas mark 2. Put the meat in a bowl and add a little salt and pepper – mix very lightly or the hamburgers will be dense and tough.

3 Divide the meat into 4 and shape into flat round burgers. Squeeze them so they don't break up when cooking.

4 Cut the buns in half and put them cut side up under the grill until toasted – don't turn them over. Take them out and keep them warm in the oven.

5 Brush the burgers lightly with oil and grill or barbecue for 4 to 6 minutes each side, depending how well done

you like them. Remember to brush the second side with a little oil when you turn them over, and do mind you don't touch any part of the grill.

6 Put the burgers into the buns, topping with onion slices, fresh tomato or sauce if you like.

VARIATIONS

1

Cheeseburgers

When the burgers are cooked, place 1 slice of processed cheese on top and grill until just melted.

2

Beefburgers

Use best lean mince instead of the steak. Mix it with 50 g (2 oz) chopped onion and 50 g (2 oz) breadcrumbs then cook as for hamburgers.

BARBECUE SAUCE

Serves 4   Medium easy

1 medium onion
1-cm (½-in) slice fresh ginger
1 clove garlic
1 large stick celery
2 tablespoons oil
150 ml (¼ pint) water
1 × 400-g (14-oz) tin chopped
   tomatoes
1 tablespoon lemon juice
1 tablespoon vinegar (wine
   vinegar is best)
2 tablespoons tomato purée
2–4 teaspoons Worcestershire
   sauce
2 tablespoons brown sugar
a pinch of dried oregano
1 large bay leaf
a pinch of salt
a pinch of nutmeg

1

 Peel and chop the onion, peel and grate the ginger, peel and crush the garlic. Cut the celery into cubes (see page 94).

2

Put the oil in a saucepan on medium heat for a minute or so, then add the onion, garlic, ginger and celery. Cook for about 5 minutes until the onion is soft but not brown.

3

Put in everything else and turn up the heat until the mixture starts to bubble. Turn down the heat and let it cook for about 45 minutes.

4

Take the pan off the heat, turn off the heat and very carefully, perhaps with help, pour the sauce through a sieve, rubbing it with a spoon to help it through. You may need to heat it up again if it takes a long time.

If you like a chunky sauce you can use it without sieving it.

FISH PARCELS

Serves 4   Medium easy

4 fish steaks (cod, salmon or whatever is available)

a little olive oil

fresh or dried herbs (dill, chives, thyme or parsley are all good)

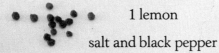 1 lemon

salt and black pepper

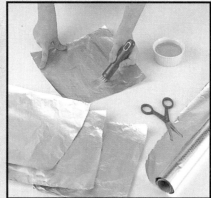

Silver foil is ideal for wrapping and cooking things on the barbecue – or in the oven – and you can prepare these parcels in advance and keep them in the fridge for a few hours until you are ready to cook them. You can judge the quantities easily and each person gets their own portion, without having any messy serving out.

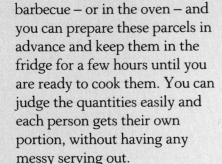

1 Turn on the oven to 180°C (350°F), gas mark 4 (or make sure the barbecue is nearly ready!).

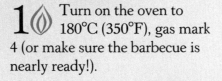

2 Cut 4 pieces of double thickness silver foil large enough to wrap up the fish steaks. Brush the *dull side* of the foil with oil.

3 Very carefully chop the fresh herbs into tiny pieces, saving a little unchopped sprigs for decorating. Cut the lemon in half, then cut one half into 4 slices, and the 4 slices into 8 half-slices. Mind your fingers – a lemon can be slippery.

— VARIATIONS —

1

Small whole fish such as trout or mackerel cook beautifully in foil. Make sure they are cleaned first (that means all the insides removed and if necessary the scales taken off; you can leave the head on if you like). The baked fish recipes on page 84 would also cook well in foil.

2

Chicken breasts are good cooked in foil. Put a spoonful of cooked rice and some sliced cooked leeks or onions on to the oiled foil (double thickness, remember) then the skinned chicken breast. Top with two half-slices of orange, wrap and bake for 30 minutes. If you cook some rice and include it in the foil with some vegetables in this way you can make a complete meal in a parcel.

4 Lay a fish steak on the foil and sprinkle some herbs on top (don't worry if you couldn't get fresh ones, dried will do fine). Add a squeeze of juice from the half lemon, some salt and pepper and a little more olive oil to each steak.

5 Wrap up the foil *loosely*, and fold over the join so it keeps the steam and flavour in. Tuck the ends underneath.

6 Put the foil parcels into the oven (don't forget to wear oven gloves) for 20 minutes, or on to the barbecue for about the same time, but turn them half-way through. Mind the steam when you unwrap them. Serve either in the foil or on serving plates, with 2 half-slices of lemon and a sprig of herbs on each one.

49

BANANAS COOKED IN THEIR SKINS

Serves 4   Easy

4 large bananas – and that's it!

This must be about the simplest hot pudding recipe in the world. The taste is quite delicious, and the fruit comes ready to cook in its own special package! Do try it.

1 Turn on the grill to high to get it hot (or have the barbecue ready).

2 Put the bananas in the grill pan (or on the barbecue) and place it carefully under the grill, the medium distance away, for about 15 minutes until the bananas are

almost black and quite soft. Turn them over occasionally, using oven gloves or tongs. Towards the end of the cooking time you must turn them very gently in case you burst them.

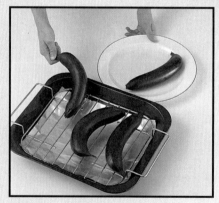

3 When the bananas are soft and black remove the grill pan and allow them to cool slightly before moving them. Use oven gloves or tongs to remove them from the barbecue. Turn off the grill.

4 They are very hot so warn your friends to be careful as they peel back the skin and eat the lovely inside. They are very good on their own, or with ice-cream, cream or chocolate sauce.

VARIATIONS

1

Chocolate Bananas

Peel the banana and lay it on a work surface. Cut a thin slice lengthways from off the top and put it to one side. Scoop a shallow trough along the cut surface of the banana – it will look a little like a curved canoe. Fill the trough with chocolate drops and replace the lid. Wrap in silver foil and grill or barbecue for 10 to 20 minutes until the banana is soft. Be careful as you unwrap them as they will be very hot.

2

Fruit Kebabs

Mix together in a jug 125 ml (4½ fl oz) orange juice, 50 ml (2 fl oz) lemon juice, 2 tablespoons clear honey and 1 teaspoon chopped fresh mint. Wash, peel and cut all sorts of fruits (banana, apple, orange or some tropical mango or pineapple) into bite-sized pieces. Put them into a large bowl and pour over the fruit juice. Let it soak (marinade) for an hour or two. Thread the fruits on to wooden skewers which have been soaked in water (to stop them burning). Include some marshmallows if you like. Brush the kebabs with a little melted butter and sprinkle with some brown sugar. Cook under the grill or on the barbecue for 6 to 8 minutes, but watch them all the time and turn them to stop them burning. Heat the marinade and serve it as a sauce.

POTATO SKINS

Makes 24   Easy

4 large potatoes

olive oil, salt

75 g (3 oz) butter

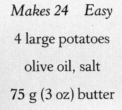

These are so delicious I know you and your friends will love them. The Americans call them 'peel-outs' and they serve them with soured cream, but if you don't like that then they are good with ketchup, melted butter or a dip. You can make them early in the day and re-heat them in the oven if you like.

1 Turn on the oven to 200°C (400°F), gas mark 6.

2 Scrub the potatoes clean, dry them well, then prick them all over with a fork. Rub the skins with a little olive oil and salt. Bake them in the oven for about an hour, or until they feel soft and cooked when you squeeze them – but don't burn your fingers.

3 Turn on the oven again to 200°C (400°F), gas mark 6.

4 When the potatoes are cold, cut them carefully in half and scoop out most of the flesh with a spoon, leaving a little bit clinging to the skin. Put the flesh in a bowl and keep to use for one of the variations. Cut the half skins into three pieces each, so you have 24 altogether.

5 Melt the butter in a little saucepan then remove it from the heat. Brush each piece of skin with the butter on both sides then put them on a baking sheet.

6 Bake them for 20 minutes, then carefully, wearing oven gloves, take them out. Serve them with a bowl of soured cream or dip.

TO GO WITH THE SKINS

1

Instead of plain soured cream, chop a little fresh chives and stir them in.

2

Mix 175 g (6 oz) cream cheese, 1 tablespoon tomato ketchup and 2 tablespoons soured cream with some salt and black pepper.

3

Mash up 1 ripe avocado with 1 tablespoon lemon juice, 2 tablespoons cream cheese and salt and black pepper.

4

Mayonnaise mixed with some crushed garlic and chopped herbs.

TO USE UP THE POTATO FLESH

Potato Balls

Mash up the cooked potato (should be about 225 g (8 oz), but it doesn't matter exactly) with 1 egg yolk, 2 teaspoons soft butter, 2 tablespoons double cream and 50 g (2 oz) cooked rice. Shape the mixture into little balls and roll them in sesame seeds, then bake them in a medium oven at 180°C (350°F), gas mark 4 for 15 minutes.

Tuna Fish Cakes

Mash up the cooked potato with 1 × 225-g (8-oz) tin tuna fish, 2 teaspoons soft butter, 1 beaten egg and salt and pepper. Shape into cakes and cover with flour or breadcrumbs. Fry the cakes in hot oil for a few minutes on each side.

To Serve Baked Potatoes

Bake the potatoes as above. When cooked, cut them open and serve with a lump of butter or a filling:
sour cream mixed with chopped fresh chives;
prawns and mayonnaise;
coleslaw;
grated carrot, chopped apple and raisins;
baked beans with bits of crispy fried bacon;
sweetcorn with chopped peppers;
tuna fish and mayonnaise;
Boursin cheese;
chopped celery, apple, walnut and mayonnaise (Waldorf salad);
thousand island or blue cheese dressing;
tomato relish.

PASTA WITH CREAM AND CHEESE

Serves 4   Easy

1 tablespoon olive oil

salt and pepper

350 g (12 oz) dried egg tagliatelle or 450 g (1 lb) fresh fettucine

200 ml (7 fl oz) crème fraiche or fromage blanc

25 g (1 oz) butter

75 g (3 oz) grated Parmesan cheese

You can now buy two different kinds of pasta – either fresh or dried. If it's cooked properly there isn't much difference in taste, but the fresh needs only to be boiled for 1 to 2 minutes while the dried takes more like 8. You can serve pasta just tossed in a little butter and cheese or, for a special occasion, with a sauce.

1 Put at least 1.75 l (3 pints) of water in a large saucepan with the oil and a pinch of salt. Put the pan on a high heat until the water is

bubbling then very carefully add the pasta, minding you don't get splashed.

2 Keep the heat high until the water starts to bubble again, then turn it down so the pasta doesn't boil over the edge. Give it a stir then let it bubble gently for about 8 minutes if it is dried or 1 to 2 minutes if it is fresh.

3 While the pasta is cooking, heat the crème fraiche or fromage blanc with the butter in a small saucepan. Add 2 tablespoons of the pasta

cooking liquid. Mix well then turn the heat low so it just keeps warm without bubbling.

4 Taste a piece of pasta to see if it is cooked – but do be careful because it will be very hot. It should not be mushy, but still have a bit of bite to it.

5 Wearing oven gloves or asking a grown-up to help, tip the pasta into a large colander, letting the hot water drain away underneath. Don't drain it too thoroughly, it should be left nice and slimy so it mixes well with the sauce. Immediately put it back in the hot pan.

6 Tip the warm crème fraiche on to the pasta and add most of the Parmesan. Mix well and put it in a warm serving dish, sprinkled with the rest of the Parmesan.

VARIATIONS

1

Tomato Sauce

The best tomatoes to use by far are the Italian or French plum tomatoes which you can buy in some supermarkets in the summer. If you can't get them use the big round 'beef' tomatoes. You need 750 g (1½ lb). First skin the tomatoes: put them in a large bowl and pour boiling water over them (perhaps a grown-up should help). Leave them for about 15 seconds, then carefully take them out with a spoon and put them in a bowl of cold water. You'll find you can easily peel off the skins. Cut them into quarters and push out and throw away the seeds. Chop the flesh you have left and cook it in a heavy frying pan with 4 tablespoons olive oil, 2 cloves garlic, peeled and chopped, 2 teaspoons tomato paste, 1 teaspoon dried oregano, and salt and black pepper. Cook it all gently for about 8 to 10 minutes until it is thickened a little. Very good with any shape of pasta. You can also make the sauce without peeling and de-seeding the tomatoes. It's not so smooth but still very tasty. Or use the sauce on page 63.

RISOTTO

Serves 4   Medium easy

1 large onion

25 g (1 oz) butter

2 tablespoons oil

350 g (12 oz) dry risotto rice

900 ml (1½ pints) stock

grated Parmesan cheese

A classic Italian dish of rice cooked slowly in stock. The result should be creamy and delicious – don't expect the separate drier grains of Indian rice. It's important that you use *risotto* rice – you can buy it in packets from most supermarkets. Once you've understood the basic principle, you can add all sorts of interesting ingredients and invent your own variations. Use a good vegetable stock cube to make the stock.

1 Skin the onion and chop it into small pieces (see page 94). Put the butter and oil in a large, heavy frying pan. Turn on a medium heat and let the butter melt. Add the onion to the pan and fry it gently (sauté) for 5 to 6 minutes until it's golden and soft.

2 Add the rice (don't wash it, there's no need to with this type of rice) and let it cook for 2 minutes. It should be a little transparent – as if you can

see through the outside of the grain but the inside is still hard and white.

3 Pour in about one-third of the stock (300 ml (½ pint)). Turn up the heat until the stock starts to bubble (boil) then turn the heat down until the liquid is not quite bubbling – just a quivering movement (this is called simmering).

4 Let it simmer until the liquid is absorbed, stirring it often. This will take about 10 to 12 minutes.

5 🔥 Add another 150 ml (¼ pint) water every 3 to 4 minutes, waiting each time until it is absorbed.

6 🔥 It should take about 25 to 30 minutes for all the liquid to be absorbed, and the rice should be fluffy, creamy and sticky yet with a touch of bite to it. Serve the risotto with Parmesan cheese to sprinkle over it.

── VARIATIONS ──

1

Risotto Milanese

🔪 🔥 When the onion is cooked add 75–100 g (3–4 oz) lean chopped bacon and let it cook. Add 100 g (4 oz) chopped mushrooms with the rice.

2

Seafood Risotto

🔥 Five minutes before the end of the cooking time add 100 g (4 oz) peeled, cooked prawns and 100 g (4 oz) cooked and drained frozen mixed vegetables (such as sweetcorn and peppers perhaps).

3

Plain Boiled Rice

🔥 Just put 300 ml (½ pint) rice into a saucepan. Add 60 ml (1 pint) boiling water or stock and 1 teaspoon oil. Turn the heat on high. When it is bubbling hard (a rolling boil) stir well once then put on a well fitting lid and turn the heat right down. It must be very low or the rice at the bottom will burn. Leave completely alone – don't stir it or even peep! After 25 minutes have a look – if all the water has gone and the rice looks tender and fluffy, it is done. If not, cook for a little longer. Brown rice takes at least 45 to 50 minutes.

BEAN AND VEGETABLE CASSEROLE

Serves 4   Medium easy

100 g (4 oz) black-eyed beans

1 good vegetable stock cube

75 g (3 oz) yellow or green lentils

2 medium onions

3 large carrots

4 sticks celery

3 cloves garlic

4 tablespoons olive oil

2 teaspoons dried marjoram or mixed herbs

2 teaspoons soy sauce

1 tablespoon tomato purée

1 teaspoon French mustard

2 teaspoons sugar

salt and pepper

This makes an excellent vegetarian main course or a very filling starter. Dried beans and peas (called pulses) are full of protein, easy to cook and delicious. It's very important that you soak them in water overnight before cooking them, and don't add salt until the end of the recipe or it makes the beans tough. All beans must be boiled for at least 10 minutes as otherwise some types can cause stomach upsets.

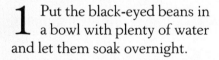

1 Put the black-eyed beans in a bowl with plenty of water and let them soak overnight.

2 Drain the beans then put in a saucepan with 1 litre (1¾ pints) water. Turn on the heat, wait until the water is bubbling then let it boil for 10 minutes. Carefully add the stock cube. Rinse the lentils in a sieve and add them too. Turn down the heat and let it bubble very gently (simmer) for 45 minutes.

3 While the beans are cooking, peel the onions, cut them in half and slice them. Wash the carrots and celery and slice them too, then wash the garlic cloves, take off the skin and chop them into tiny bits (see page 94).

4 Put the olive oil in a large heavy frying pan or a casserole and heat it gently. Add all the vegetables and the herbs and stir every now and then while they cook gently for about 10 minutes.

5 When the beans are cooked, add them with their stock to the vegetables – be very careful, perhaps a grown-up should do this. Stir in the soy sauce, tomato purée, French mustard and sugar and let it all go on cooking gently for another 20 minutes, stirring every now and then. Very carefully (it'll be hot) taste a little to see if it needs salt and pepper.

see page 94

VARIATION

1 To make a pie instead of a casserole, make a cheesy potato topping: Carefully peel and cut up 750 g (1½ lb) potatoes. Cook in boiling water until tender (about 20 minutes) then drain carefully. Mash up with a little milk and butter until all the lumps have gone, then mix with 75 g (3 oz) grated cheese, a little salt and pepper and a pinch of mustard powder. Make the casserole as above, but only add about 300 ml (¾ pint) of the bean stock to the vegetables. You can either spread the topping on the vegetables with a fork, or pipe it on through a piping bag and large rosette nozzle. Sprinkle with a little extra cheese and bake for 30 minutes at 180°C (350°F), gas mark 4.

PORK IN APPLE JUICE

Serves 4   Medium easy

2 tablespoons oil

500 g (1¼ lb) lean casserole pork, cut in cubes (your butcher may do this for you)

1 medium onion

1 clove garlic

1 large eating apple

1 medium cooking apple

1 teaspoon sugar

½ teaspoon dried thyme (or a sprig of fresh)

200 ml (7 fl oz) apple juice

200 ml (7 fl oz) stock, made from a good vegetable stock cube, or water

salt and pepper

There is a classic recipe for pork cooked in cider but I think using apple juice is even better. The good thing about this kind of dish – called a casserole – is that you can make it and put it into the oven very early, so that everything can be cleared up and ready by the time your friends arrive.

1 Turn on the oven to 180°C (350°F), gas mark 4. Put the oil in a large saucepan. Heat for a minute or so on a medium heat. Put in the pork and fry it for a few minutes, turning it so all sides get golden brown. Mind the hot oil doesn't spit at you (that's why a saucepan is better than a frying pan) and do keep going until it is really brown – this may take up to 10 minutes. Take it out with a spoon with holes in it (to leave the oil in the pan) and put it in an ovenproof casserole dish.

2 Peel the onion and slice it thinly. Peel and slice the garlic (see page 94). Wash the apples and cut in quarters. Cut out the cores then chop into 1-cm (½-in) cubes. Mind your fingers.

3 Fry the onion and garlic for about 5 minutes then take them out with the slotted spoon and add them to the meat.

4 Fry the apple cubes for a minute or so then put them into the casserole too. Add the sugar and thyme then mix it all well together.

5 Carefully pour the apple juice and stock (or water) into the saucepan. Add a little salt and pepper, stir well, turn up the heat until the liquid is bubbling, then *very* carefully, perhaps with help, pour it over the pork and apple mixture. (When you collect all the meat juices and tasty bits from a pan by boiling some liquid in it in this way, it's called deglazing the pan.)

6 Cover the casserole then put it carefully in the oven for about 1½ hours.

7 If you have used fresh thyme remember to remove the stalk before serving. This would be lovely served with rice or noodles or mashed potato and a green vegetable.

VARIATIONS

1

You can very easily make a delicious casserole from lamb and apricots. Cut 750 g (1½ lb) neck fillet, leg or shoulder of lamb into cubes (the butcher will do this for you). Brown the lamb with 1 large chopped onion and 2 tablespoons oil in a heavy saucepan for 5 to 6 minutes until the lamb is really brown. Put it into a casserole and add 600 ml (1 pint) stock, made from good vegetable stock powder, ½ teaspoon cinnamon, salt and pepper, 1 tablespoon lemon juice and 175 g (6 oz) semi-dried ready-to-eat apricots. Cover and cook for 1¼ hours at 190°C (375°F), gas mark 5, then (carefully!) take it out. Stir in 1 tablespoon apricot jam, then taste – remember it's very hot – and if you think it needs it add a squeeze of lemon juice. Serve with rice (see page 57).

WHITE SAUCE

Makes 450 ml (¾ pint)   Easy

40 g (1½ oz) butter

25 g (1 oz) plain flour

450 ml (¾ pint) milk

salt and black pepper

Many sauces are based on a white sauce. The traditional way of making one is to add the liquid bit by bit to a cooked flour and butter mixture (called a roux), but it can be quite tricky. For the last few years I have used this all-in-one method that I learnt from Delia Smith, one of my favourite cooks. It has a very slightly different taste from the classic method, but it's very simple and quick and makes a lovely smooth sauce.

1 Put the butter, flour and milk into a saucepan. Try to use one with a good, flat, thick bottom.

2 Put the saucepan on a medium heat and whisk everything together firmly with a wire whisk. Keep going, and as the sauce gets hot it will begin to bubble and thicken (this is one of the magic moments of cookery).

3 Scrape round the bottom of the saucepan with a wooden spoon then whisk hard again. Don't worry if there are lumps; keep whisking and you can get rid of them (and if the worst comes to the worst you can always put it through a sieve – we've all had to do that sometimes).

4 Turn the heat down and let the sauce go on cooking for 6 minutes, stirring occasionally.

5 Add a little salt and pepper (some people use white pepper, as they don't like black specks, but I much prefer the taste of black pepper) – and that's it! To make a cheese sauce, simply stir in 75 g (3 oz) of grated cheese at this stage.

VARIATIONS

1

The all-in-one sauce also works brilliantly in the microwave. Put everything in a large glass bowl – at least twice as big as the amount of milk – and cook it on full power for 6 to 7 minutes, *whisking very well once each minute.* It really does work: don't panic the first few times you whisk it as you feel big lumps at the bottom, they will all disappear if you whisk hard enough.

2

Parsley Sauce
Stir 2 tablespoons chopped parsley into the cooked sauce.

3

Onion Sauce
Cook 1 large chopped onion in the milk for a few minutes then let it get completely cold in the fridge before making the sauce as above.

TOMATO SAUCE

1 small onion
1 clove garlic
1½ tablespoons olive oil
1 × 400-g (14-oz) tin chopped
   Italian tomatoes
½ teaspoon sugar
150 ml (¼ pint) red wine or
   stock
2 teaspoons tomato purée
a pinch of dried oregano
salt and pepper
1 small bay leaf

1

Carefully chop the onion very finely. Peel and slice the garlic (see page 94).

2

Put the oil in a saucepan or large frying pan. Put it on a medium heat and add the onion and garlic. Cook for 3 to 4 minutes until the onion is soft.

3

Add everything else and turn up the heat until the mixture starts to bubble. Turn down the heat and let the sauce cook gently – tiny bubbles around the edge – without a lid (this is called simmering).

4

Let it go on simmering very gently for about 25 minutes, stirring every now and then. The liquid will slowly disappear, and the sauce will get thicker and stronger tasting (this is called reducing).

5

Now you can press the sauce through a sieve with a spoon (or put it in the blender or processor) if you want it smooth, or use it as it is. Or you can use the tomato sauce on page 55.

MIXED SALAD

Serves 4   Easy   No cook

1 lettuce

4 ripe tomatoes

about ⅓ cucumber

½ green pepper

½ red pepper

Almost anything can be served with a side salad instead of a vegetable, or you can make a more filling salad by adding pulses like tinned red kidney beans, or by using potatoes, rice or pasta. Many vegetables are delicious eaten raw – my children have always preferred uncooked carrot, peas and cabbage. Don't use too many things at once; it's usually better to stick to 3 or 4 ingredients, and think a little about the colours when you decide what to put together. It's important that you don't get a salad ready too far ahead, as the ingredients can go limp and soggy.

1 Choose good fresh lettuce – if you like it crunchy buy Cos, Webbs or Iceberg. Pull the leaves apart and give them a good wash.

2 Put the lettuce in a tea towel, wrap it up gently, then whirl it round your head outside (preferably) to get it as dry as possible.

3 Wash the tomatoes and pull off the stalks. If you want to be really smart you can peel them but (see page 55) it's usually not worth bothering. Carefully cut them into quarters or slice them.

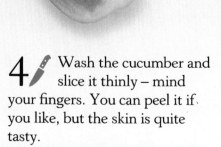

4 Wash the cucumber and slice it thinly – mind your fingers. You can peel it if you like, but the skin is quite tasty.

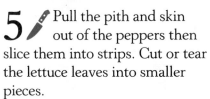

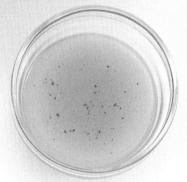

5  Pull the pith and skin out of the peppers then slice them into strips. Cut or tear the lettuce leaves into smaller pieces.

6 Gently arrange the salad in a serving bowl. Keep it in the fridge until you are ready to serve, then pour over some dressing (see right) and mix it up very carefully.

OTHER SALADS

1

Add chopped avocado, raw mushrooms and a few walnuts to a green salad.

2

Put some cubes of Feta cheese and some black olives on top of a salad of Cos lettuce and tomato – a delicious Greek salad.

3

Tomato and Mozarella Salad

A good starter or side salad. For each person: cut 1 large tomato (a plum tomato is best of all) and half a lump of Mozarella cheese into thin slices. Arrange them prettily on a side plate, then pour over a little good olive oil and if possible sprinkle with some fresh chopped basil. If you can't get any, use a little bit of dried Italian herbs.

DRESSINGS

1

Vinaigrette
A good vinaigrette dressing is simply 1 part white wine vinegar to 3 to 5 parts olive oil – depending how sharp you like it – plus salt and black pepper. You can replace some or all of the vinegar with lemon juice, and experiment by adding crushed garlic, mustard, sugar and herbs. You need to mix it very well just before you use it, as it separates when left to stand. You can try different oils in salad dressings: sesame, walnut and so on.

2

If you haven't time to make your own mayonnaise, use one of the good ready-made ones: you could add a pinch of curry or saffron powder, a dash of tomato ketchup, some garlic or herbs to make a change.

— CHOCOLATE FONDUE —

Serves 4   Easy

5 tablespoons single cream

40 g (1½ oz) cocoa powder

100 g (4 oz) caster sugar

175 g (6 oz) golden syrup

25 g (1 oz) butter

a pinch of salt

a few drops of vanilla essence

A fondue is a bowl of hot sauce in which you dip food on the end of forks. You can have a meat fondue, where pieces of steak are dipped in hot oil to cook them, then served with a variety of sauces, or a cheese fondue for dipping pieces of bread, but the most delicious of all is this chocolate one. It is easy to make, but there must be a grown-up around when you make this, as the mixture gets extremely hot when it is boiling, and is very dangerous.

1 ◊ Put everything except the vanilla essence in a large saucepan. Mix well. Put the saucepan on a high heat and let the mixture get hotter and hotter while you keep stirring.

2 ◊ When it starts to bubble do be very careful. Let it keep bubbling hard (boiling) while you stir every now and then. As it boils it will get slowly thicker.

3 ◊ When you think the sauce is thick enough to dip the fruit in without being too drippy, take the pan very

carefully off the heat. Add the vanilla essence and stir. Let it cool a little before serving so it doesn't burn anyone's mouth.

VARIATION

1

This sauce cooks easily and well in a microwave. You must use a bowl at least 3 to 4 times bigger than the amount of sauce, as it boils up in the oven. Put everything except the vanilla in the bowl, mix well and cook on full power for 3 minutes, stirring once each minute. You must wear oven gloves when touching the bowl, as it will get very hot. Then cook on full power for 3 to 5 minutes, stirring once. If it's still not thick enough cook for another minute or so. Add the vanilla and mix well, then let it cool a little before serving.

4 Use about 175 g (6 oz) fruit for each person, cut in bite-sized pieces. Choose from apples, pears, pineapple, starfruit, oranges, bananas, grapes, strawberries, peaches and so on.

5 Put the chocolate mixture in a serving bowl and, using forks or wooden skewers, dip the fruit into it piece by piece. If the sauce gets too cold and thick you may have to put the bowl over a pan of hot water to reheat it.

TIRAMI SU

Serves 4   Easy   No cook

4 trifle sponges

3 tablespoons Camp coffee

3 tablespoons water

225 g (8 oz) crème fraiche or Greek yoghurt

50 g (2 oz) double cream

1 tablespoon caster sugar

1 teaspoon vanilla sugar (or a few drops vanilla essence)

1–2 tablespoons cocoa powder

The name of this Italian pudding means 'lift me up' or 'pick me up' in English, but the genuine version is so rich I think it's more likely to make you fall asleep. It should really be made with a very rich creamy cheese called mascarpone, egg yolk and liqueur, but I make a lighter, easier kind which is just as tasty. I think your friends will love it.

1 Carefully slice the trifle sponges in half across and use your fingers to press one half of each into little individual dishes.

2 Mix the Camp coffee with the water in a little bowl. Pour 1 dessertspoonful over each half sponge and let it soak in.

3 Mix the crème fraiche or yoghurt with the cream, caster sugar and vanilla sugar in a medium-sized bowl. Stir it very hard with a fork until it gets a bit thicker and creamier (this is called beating).

4 With a spoon use half the cream mixture to put a layer over each sponge.

5 Dip the other sponge halves in the coffee/water mixture that you have left, and put them on top of the cream mixture. Finish with another layer of cream.

6 Put the dishes in the fridge. Just before serving, sprinkle the tops with cocoa powder through a little sieve (perhaps your tea strainer).

VARIATIONS

1

If you would like to make this for grown-ups (and it would make a wonderful pudding for a special celebration) you could still use this recipe, as most people nowadays prefer not to eat too much cream and egg yolk, but it would be lovely to add a little liqueur. Only use 1 tablespoon water and add 1 tablespoon Tia Maria or Kahlua (they are both coffee-tasting).

2

The nearest English recipe to tirami su is trifle. Just use fruit juice to soak the sponges rather than coffee and use custard instead of the cream mixture. You can put fruit into the trifle if you like, and decorate with whipped cream and cherries.

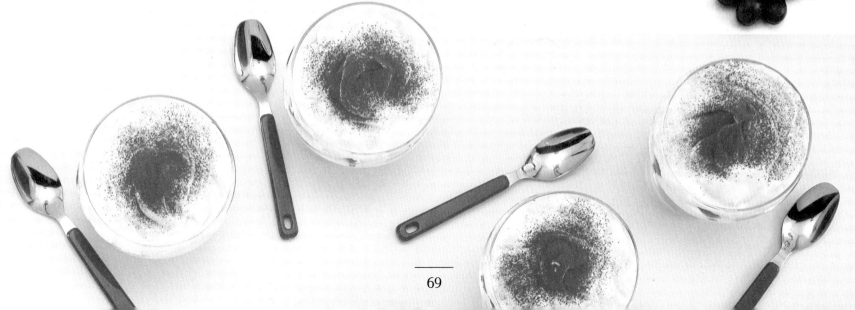

ICE-CREAM

Serves at least 4   Easy   No cook

600 ml (1 pint) whipping cream

175 g (6 oz) caster sugar

1 teaspoon vanilla essence

Home-made ice-cream is delicious. The problem is that ice crystals can form while it's freezing, especially if the freezer isn't very cold. It's best made in the special machines that stir it and freeze it at the same time, but they're very expensive. If you make a rich mixture like this one it will only need stirring a couple of times during freezing, and tastes wonderful.

1 Turn the freezer on to its lowest setting 2 to 3 hours before starting to make the ice-cream. Put a mixing bowl and a plastic box into the freezer to chill them before you start.

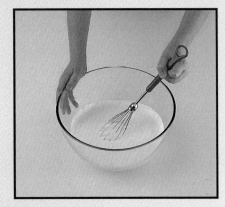

2 Put the cream into a large mixing bowl. Whip it up by beating very hard and fast with a large whisk until it is thick and fluffy. Don't beat it for too long or it will start to go lumpy and eventually separate (you'll make butter!).

3 Gently mix in the caster sugar and vanilla essence then turn the mixture into the cold box. Put it in the freezer for a couple of hours until half frozen. Mind you never touch the freezer with wet hands or your skin can stick to it.

4 Take the box out of the freezer, empty the mixture into a cold bowl and whisk it very thoroughly until it is smooth again. Return it to the box and freeze it for another hour or so.

5 Empty the mixture into the cold bowl again and whisk once more. Return it to the box and freeze it until hard – about 3 to 4 hours.

6 Before serving the ice-cream, take it out of the freezer and put it in the main part of the fridge for 30 to 40 minutes, or it will be too hard. They call this 'ripening' the ice-cream.

VARIATIONS

1

Chocolate Ice-Cream
Make the same as for vanilla, but only use ½ teaspoon vanilla essence, and stir in 200 g (7 oz) melted plain chocolate drops or broken up plain chocolate.

2

Mint Choc Chip Ice-Cream
Use peppermint essence instead of vanilla. Add 100 g (4 oz) chocolate flakes when you stir in the sugar.

3

Tutti Frutti
When you add the sugar, stir in 175 g (6 oz) chopped glacé cherries – red, green and yellow if possible – and any other glacé fruits you can get: angelica, glacé pineapple and so on. You could also add a few raisins.

SAUCES

Strawberry or raspberry: Purée 175–225 g (6–8 oz) ripe fruit with a fork or in a blender or processor and add a little sieved icing sugar.

Chocolate: Pour 1 small tin of evaporated milk into a saucepan. Carefully heat the milk until it is bubbling, then take it off the heat and stir in 175 g (6 oz) plain or milk chocolate drops. Keep stirring until the sauce is smooth and shiny. Add a few drops of vanilla essence.

Butterscotch: Put 50 g (2 oz) butter, 4 tablespoons brown sugar and 2 tablespoons golden syrup in a saucepan and stir over a gentle heat until the sugar is dissolved. Turn up the heat until it bubbles, then let it boil for 1 minute. Be very careful – hot sugar is dangerous. Add a squeeze of lemon juice and some chopped nuts if you like. Let it cool a little before serving.

CHEESE NIBBLES

Makes about 40 tiny biscuits   *Medium easy*

100 g (4 oz) self-raising flour

50 g (2 oz) butter

50 g (2 oz) strong Cheddar cheese

½ teaspoon dry mustard powder

salt and pepper

1 egg (size 3)

You might want to give a small party and need some little things that people can eat with their fingers, or if you are planning a lunch or dinner, sometimes it's good to have things to nibble before the meal. In any case, all these recipes are quick to make and delicious to eat – some of them would do to take for break at school, or in your lunch box.

1 Turn on the oven to 180°C (350°F), gas mark 4. Put the flour in a medium-sized bowl. Cut the butter in small pieces into the bowl – you needn't use a very sharp knife. Pick up small handfuls and rub the lumps of butter together with the flour between your thumbs and fingers, letting it fall back into the bowl as you do it. Keep on picking up handfuls and gently smoothing them like this until all the big lumps have gone (this is called rubbing in).

2 Grate the cheese on the large side of the grater, being very careful of your fingers, especially when you get to the last little bit.

3 Add the cheese, mustard and some salt and pepper to the bowl and mix with a spoon.

4 Break the egg into a cup and beat it with a fork. Measure 2 tablespoons egg and add it to the bowl of flour mixture. Keep any left-over egg for later.

5 Mix it all well with a fork – don't worry if it looks as if it will never join together, it will. Sprinkle the work surface with a little flour and turn the mixture on to it. Squeeze it together gently with your hands until it is all smooth (this is called kneading lightly). If you still think it's too dry and crumbly, add a little more egg.

6 Wrap the mixture – now called dough – in cling film and put it in the fridge for 30 minutes. Turn on the oven to 180°C (350°F), gas mark 4. Sprinkle the work surface and a rolling pin with flour, unwrap

the dough and knead it a little more. Roll it out to about 5 mm (¼ in) thick. Cut it into little shapes and brush the tops with left-over egg.

7 Put the biscuits on baking sheets and put them carefully in the oven for 12 to 15 minutes or until the tops are golden brown. Wearing oven gloves, take the baking sheets out of the oven and put them down somewhere heatproof. Move the biscuits on to a wire rack to cool – but mind your fingers, they'll be very hot.

VARIATIONS

1

Chive Biscuits
Use self-raising wholemeal flour instead of white, and add 1 bunch of chives, carefully chopped with scissors, instead of the cheese.

2

Things on sticks make good nibbles, but you don't have to keep to the usual cheese and pineapple. Try squares of Brie with grapes, or little pieces of melon wrapped in prosciutto (Italian ham).

3

Little cherry tomatoes are delicious and easy to eat if you scoop out the middle and fill them with Boursin or herb cream cheese.

LEEK AND POTATO SOUP

Serves 4   Easy

3 large leeks

1 large potato (or 2 medium ones)

1 onion

50 g (2 oz) butter

900 ml (1½ pints) water or chicken stock

salt and pepper

1 tablespoon cream

chopped fresh parsley or chives

A soup makes a wonderful starter for a special meal, and a home-made leek and potato is one of the best; thick, warming and easy to make. If you add some cream and serve it cold it's called 'Vichyssoise'. Do try the minestrone soup as well – not the same at all as the tinned sort which, although good and comforting in its own way, has a completely different taste.

1 Cut the root ends off the leeks and take off any tough leaves. Slice them very thinly and wash them carefully in a sieve, as they may be quite

earthy and gritty. Peel the potato and onion and chop them into little pieces (see page 94).

2 Put the butter in a large saucepan and melt it over a medium heat. Add all the vegetables, stir them to mix with the butter then put the lid on the pan and turn the heat down. Let them cook very gently for about 15 minutes.

3 Add the water or stock and turn up the heat. When it is just starting to bubble, put the lid on again and

turn the heat right down. Let it cook very gently for about 20 minutes.

can splash) pour the soup into a blender and whizz it up until it's smooth. Or press it all through a sieve with a wooden spoon.

5 Pour the soup back into the saucepan and heat it up again, adding a little salt and pepper. When you pour it in the soup bowls you can dribble a little cream on top, then sprinkle on some chopped fresh chives or parsley.

4 When the vegetables are soft, carefully (it may be best to let a grown-up do it as it

VARIATIONS

1

Microwave Version
Cook the vegetables in the butter on full power for 10 minutes. Add the water (or stock) and cook on full power for a further 12 minutes.

2

Minestrone Soup
Shred 100 g (4 oz) cabbage, cut 175 g (6 oz) potato into small dice, peel and chop 50 g (2 oz) onion, slice 100 g (4 oz) carrot thinly, slice 75 g (3 oz) leeks into rings and slice 75 g (3 oz) celery (see page 94). Put 25 g (1 oz) butter in a large saucepan and melt it over a medium heat. Add all the vegetables and 1 × 400-g (14-oz) tin of tomatoes. Cook the vegetables, stirring every now and then, until they are quite soft – about 10 minutes. Stir in 900 ml (1½ pints) stock, 2 teaspoons tomato purée and salt and pepper. Turn up the heat until the soup starts to bubble, then turn it right down and put the lid on. Let it cook for about 10 minutes, then add 50 g (2 oz) tiny pasta shapes. Let it simmer for another 10 minutes or so until the pasta is cooked. Serve sprinkled with grated Parmesan cheese.

—BAKED CHICKEN BREASTS—

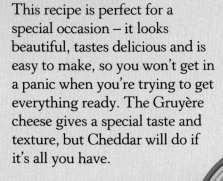

Serves 4   Medium easy

4 chicken breasts (buy the ones without bones)

salt and black pepper

1 clove garlic

1 × 275-g (10-oz) tin sliced mushrooms
(or cooked fresh ones are even better)

a pinch of dried oregano

a pinch of dried thyme

1 × 425-g (15-oz) tin chopped Italian tomatoes

50 g (2 oz) Gruyère cheese

3 tablespoon fresh breadcrumbs

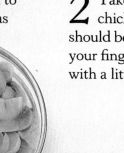

This recipe is perfect for a special occasion – it looks beautiful, tastes delicious and is easy to make, so you won't get in a panic when you're trying to get everything ready. The Gruyère cheese gives a special taste and texture, but Cheddar will do if it's all you have.

1 ⬦ Turn on the oven to 180°C (350°F), gas mark 4.

2 Take the skin off the chicken breasts – you should be able to pull it off with your fingers. Sprinkle the breasts with a little salt and pepper.

1

Vegetables

 Serve the chicken with something green to make a good colour contrast. 250 g (8 oz) of one of these would be enough for 4:

Mangetouts: Pull off the top and tail with your fingers. Wash. Cook very quickly in boiling water for 2 to 3 minutes if you like them crunchy (I do). Drain carefully and put a little butter on top.

French Beans: The same as mangetouts but cook a little longer until tender but still with a bite to them.

Broccoli: Cut off the hard bit at the bottom of the stalks. Cut into small pieces then put into boiling water stalks downwards for 4 to 5 minutes. Don't overcook – it should still be very green and a little crunchy.

3 Carefully take the skin off the garlic and chop it into tiny bits (see page 94). Put the chicken breasts into a greased (or oiled) ovenproof dish and put the drained mushrooms and chopped garlic on top.

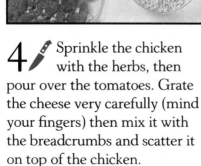

4 Sprinkle the chicken with the herbs, then pour over the tomatoes. Grate the cheese very carefully (mind your fingers) then mix it with the breadcrumbs and scatter it on top of the chicken.

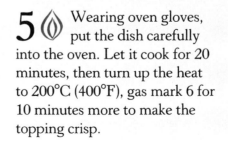

5 Wearing oven gloves, put the dish carefully into the oven. Let it cook for 20 minutes, then turn up the heat to 200°C (400°F), gas mark 6 for 10 minutes more to make the topping crisp.

77

FILO CHICKEN PIE

Serves 4   Advanced

1 small cooked chicken

175 g (6 oz) soft cream cheese

150 ml (¼ pint) double cream

salt and black pepper

1 × 275-g (10-oz) tin sliced mushrooms (or cooked fresh ones)

olive oil

6 sheets filo pastry (don't open the packet till you're ready to use it)

Filo is very thin, flaky Greek pastry that you buy ready-made in packets from the supermarket. Most recipes tell you to brush melted butter between every sheet, but that makes it very rich and it's not a good idea to eat too much butter. I have found using olive oil works just as well. You can fill filo with savoury or sweet fillings and it always looks magnificent, especially if you make a large pie as a centrepiece.

1 Turn on the oven to 180°C (350°F), gas mark 4.

2 Carefully take all the meat off the chicken and shred it with a knife.

3 Mix the cream cheese, double cream, parsley and salt and pepper in a medium-sized bowl. Open the tin of mushrooms – mind your fingers – and strain off the liquid. Stir the mushrooms and chicken into the cheese mixture.

4 It's best to use a loose-bottomed 23-cm (9-in) cake tin for this, but if you haven't got one just use an ordinary tin about the same size. Brush the tin with olive oil. Open the packet of filo and take out 6 sheets, putting the rest back in the plastic wrapping in the fridge. Cover 5 sheets with a damp cloth while you work on the sixth. Brush the top side of the sheet with oil and put it in the bottom of the tin with the extra flopping over the edge. Do

the same thing with four more sheets of filo. Put the chicken mixture into the tin on the pastry and fold the extra pastry over the top. Brush with oil.

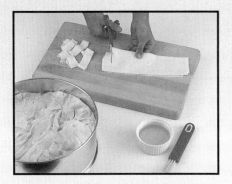

5 Brush the last sheet with oil, cut it into strips and crumple them on top of the pie.

6 Bake for 20 minutes then carefully take it out of the oven. Put it on something high and narrow, such as a narrower cake tin, so that you can let the side of the tin fall down. Bake for 15 to 20 minutes more without the side until golden brown. If you're using an ordinary tin just cook it for 35 minutes until it is golden brown on top.

VARIATIONS

1

You can use filo to make little triangles instead of one large pie. To make enough for 4: turn on the oven to 180°C (350°F), gas mark 4. Count out 4 sheets of filo and put the rest back in the packet in the fridge. Keep 3 sheets covered with a damp cloth while you work on the fourth one. Brush it with olive oil then cut it into 4 long thin strips. Lay a teaspoon of the filling in one corner of the strip and fold the corner over to make a triangle. Fold the strip over again and again, each time making a triangle. Brush with oil as you wrap, sticking down the ends, and place on a baking sheet. Do the same with the other sheets then bake for 15 to 20 minutes until golden brown.

FILLINGS

Spinach
Defrost 225 g (8 oz) frozen chopped spinach in a saucepan over a medium heat, stirring until all the liquid has gone then mix in 25 g (1 oz) butter, 120 g (4 oz) cream cheese and some salt and black pepper.

Mushroom
Wash and chop up 225 g (8 oz) mushrooms then fry them gently in 25 g (1 oz) butter for about 10 minutes until all the liquid has gone. Mix with 120 g (4 oz) cream cheese and salt and black pepper or process it until smooth.

Smoked Mackerel
Take the skin off 2 fillets of smoked mackerel and break them up in a medium-sized bowl with a fork. Mix with 50 g (2 oz) cream cheese, 2 teaspoons lemon juice and a little black pepper.

TERIYAKI

Serves 4   Easy

450 g (1 lb) best steak

2.5-cm (1-in) piece fresh stem ginger

1 clove garlic

4 spring onions

1 tablespoon soft brown sugar

120 ml (4 fl oz) dark soy sauce

1 tablespoon red wine vinegar

black pepper

1 tablespoon oil

a little oil for brushing

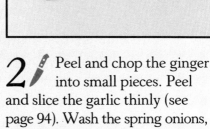

This is a Japanese way of soaking meat in a special sauce before cooking it ('marinading' the meat) which makes it tender and delicious. It's important to use fresh ginger – the dried doesn't taste the same at all – and you can now find it in most good supermarkets or greengrocers. Serve teriyaki with a green salad and rice (page 57) and it makes a very elegant meal.

1 Cut the steak into bite-sized cubes with a sharp knife – do mind your fingers.

2 Peel and chop the ginger into small pieces. Peel and slice the garlic thinly (see page 94). Wash the spring onions, cut off the tops then slice thinly.

3 Put everything except the meat into a shallow dish and mix very well with a fork. Add the meat and let it marinade for at least 2 hours, 3 to 4 if possible. Stir it every now and then. While the meat is marinading get your skewers ready: if you are using wooden ones they must be soaked in water to stop them burning.

4 Thread the meat on to the skewers, brush them with a little oil and put them under the grill or on the barbecue for about 5 minutes. Turn them half-way through and brush the other sides with oil, but do be very careful not to touch any part of the grill with your hands. If it's good beef you can serve it pink inside.

─ VARIATIONS ─

1

Chicken Teriyaki
Use 4 breasts of chicken cut into cubes. Marinade them in this mixture:

2 tablespoons clear honey
120 ml (4 fl oz) dark soy sauce
½ teaspoon salt
black pepper
1 cm (½ in) slice fresh ginger
1 clove garlic
1 tablespoon oil

Prepare the marinade and cook the chicken in the same way as for the beef, but do remember that chicken must be thoroughly cooked all the way through – about 10 minutes cooking.

2

Spare Ribs
Use 750 g (1½ lb) spare ribs and marinade them in this mixture:

½ teaspoon five flavour spice powder
2 tablespoons dark soy sauce
3 tablespoons hot water
1 tablespoon clear honey
1½ teaspoons sugar
black pepper
2–3 cloves garlic
salt

Prepare the marinade (the hot water will help the honey to soften and mix in) then put it in a roasting tin with the separated ribs for 4 to 6 hours, turning every now and then. Cook the ribs at 200°C (400°F), gas mark 6 in the marinade for 45 minutes, then very carefully move the ribs on to a roasting rack over a tin and roast for another 45 minutes.

BEEF TACOS

Serves 4   Medium easy

1 small onion

1 clove garlic

a little oil for frying

300 g (11 oz) minced beef

2 teaspoons flour

2 teaspoons tomato purée

120 ml (4 fl oz) hot stock, made from a
good stock cube, or water

8 taco shells

You can buy tacos (large folded
over Mexican crisps) ready-
made from the supermarket.

1 Turn on the oven to
180°C (350°F), gas
mark 4. Cut the top off the
onion with a sharp knife, peel off
the brown skin and chop it up
into tiny bits. Peel the clove of
garlic and slice it very thinly (see
page 94).

2 Heat the oil in a
medium-sized frying
pan and cook the onion and
garlic in it for about 5 minutes,
but don't let the garlic burn. Be
very careful that the oil doesn't
spit; keep the heat at medium
and make sure a grown-up is
watching.

3 Add the beef and cook
it, stirring, until it is
brown.

4 Sprinkle in the flour and stir well. Mix the tomato purée with the hot stock and pour it carefully into the pan – mind it doesn't splash.

5 As soon as the mixture is bubbling, turn down the heat and let it cook for 15 to 20 minutes. You'll find the liquid will partly disappear (this is called reducing and makes it thicker and stronger tasting).

6 Heat the taco shells in the oven for 2 to 3 minutes, fill them with the mince meat then add your toppings.

VARIATIONS

1

Toppings
Shredded lettuce;
soured cream;
avocado – either sliced or
    mashed up with some
    lemon juice;
grated cheese;
sliced tomato;
ketchup or relishes.

2

Instead of beef you could also fill your tacos with chopped cooked chicken mixed with mayonnaise, or make completely vegetarian ones filled with tinned drained beans under the toppings. Try some ideas of your own – almost anything makes a good filling!

BAKED FISH

Serves 4   Easy

Ask your fishmonger to give you enough fish for 4 people. You may need a fish each or just one large one. Ask him to clean and scale the fish for you – this means taking out the insides and the scales off – but to leave on the head.

75 g (3 oz) bread (to make crumbs)

a few sprigs of parsley

1 clove garlic

salt and pepper

1 lemon

1½ tablespoons olive oil

You can buy all sorts of delicious fresh fish very easily nowadays. You don't have to stuff the fish – you can just brush it with oil and bake it plain. A whole baked fish looks very spectacular and is easy to cook. Suitable fish are: bream, carp, herring, mackerel, mullet and trout. Serve with a sauce such as tomato and oregano (see page 55).

1 Turn on the oven to 190°C (375°F), gas mark 5.

2 Grate the bread very carefully on the large side of a grater, to make crumbs. If the bread is fresh it may be difficult – a blender does the job wonderfully, but you must ask a grown-up to help.

3 Very carefully chop the parsley, including the stalks, with a sharp knife. Skin the garlic and chop it into very small pieces. Mix the parsley, garlic and breadcrumbs in a small bowl and add a little salt and pepper. Take about a third of the mixture out and put it on one side.

4 Cut the lemon in half – mind your fingers – and squeeze the juice from one half into the crumb mixture, taking out any pips that fall in. Mix with a spoon.

5 Stuff the crumb, parsley and lemon mixture into the belly of the fish with your fingers.

6 Brush a baking tin or dish with oil. Put the fish in and pour some more oil over it – about 1 tablespoon. Squeeze the other half of the lemon over the fish, then sprinkle it with the crumbs and parsley that you have put aside.

7 Carefully put the dish in the oven and cook it for 45 minutes to 1 hour for a large fish, 20 to 30 minutes for small ones. When the fish is cooked, you can decorate it with some lemon and parsley.

CHINESE FISH

Rub 1 teaspoon salt and 1 tablespoon chopped ginger into the outside of the fish and put some inside as well. Leave for 30 minutes. Mix 1 teaspoon sugar, 1½ tablespoons dark soy sauce, 2 teaspoons wine vinegar, 1 tablespoon oil and 1 teaspoon sesame oil in a shallow dish. Slash the sides of the fish with a knife (careful!) and put it in the mixture to soak (marinade) for 30 minutes to 1 hour. Put it in an ovenproof or microwaveable dish or in a steamer. Sprinkle with 2 to 3 spring onions cut into matchstick shapes, 1 slice of shredded cooked ham, 2 Chinese mushrooms soaked and sliced (if possible, don't worry if you can't get them) and a little coriander. Bake in the oven as before, or steam for 15 to 20 minutes or cover with microwaveable cling film and cook on full power for 5 minutes.

OVEN-COOKED POTATOES

Serves 4   Easy

50 g (2 oz) butter

750 g (1½ lb) potatoes

1 large onion

300 ml (½ pint) hot stock made from a good stock cube

150 ml (¼ pint) milk

salt and black pepper

Most vegetables can be perfectly cooked by putting them into boiling water (careful!) and letting them simmer (that means turning down the heat so the water is slightly bubbling round the edge) until they are soft enough to eat but not mushy. Many people overcook vegetables; most – not potatoes – should still have a crunchy bite to them. To make them special serve them with a sauce (page 62).

1 Turn on the oven to 180°C (350°F), gas mark 4. Rub a large, shallow roasting tin or baking dish with half the butter.

2 Peel the potatoes. You can use a sharp knife but it's safer with a special peeler, but you still have to be careful. Cut the peeled potatoes in thin slices, but do mind your fingers.

3 Peel the onion, cut in half and slice it thinly (see page 94).

4 Put the potato and onion slices into the dish in layers, adding a little salt and pepper each time and ending up with a neat layer of potatoes.

5 Put the rest of the butter all over the top in little pieces, then pour in the hot stock and the milk.

6 Carefully put the dish in the oven and bake for 50 minutes to 1 hour until the top is brown. You can then turn down the heat and keep the potatoes warm for at least 30 minutes.

1

Braised Leeks and Tomatoes

Braised means cooked in a little liquid in the oven. Turn on the oven to 180°C (350°F), gas mark 4. Take the outside leaves off the leeks and cut off the tough end pieces. Slice the rest carefully into 2-cm (¾-in) pieces and wash very well under running water to get out all the earth. Put the slices into a buttered ovenproof dish. Open a 400-g (14-oz) tin Italian tomatoes and put them in a bowl. Break up the tomatoes with a fork then pour them over the leeks with their juice and with 3 cloves garlic, peeled and chopped and a little salt and black pepper. Cover the dish with foil and cook for 30 minutes, then uncover it and sprinkle the top with 25 g (1 oz) grated Cheddar cheese. Put it back in the oven without a cover for 10 minutes.

2

Puréed Vegetables

If you have a blender or food processor, puréed vegetables are very easy, look wonderful and can be cooked ahead of time and kept warm. Cook the vegetables in boiling water – perhaps a grown-up should help – then drain them. Add a little cream, butter and salt and pepper and blend or process until smooth. All sorts of vegetables, or mixtures of vegetables, can be puréed: broccoli, sprouts, carrot and parsnip, leek and celeriac and so on.

FRUIT BRULÉE

Serves 4   Easy

2 oranges

1 small bunch black grapes

2 kiwi fruit

6 apricots (or use any other fruit you like –
strawberries, bananas, apples and so on)

juice of ½ lemon

50 g (2 oz) double cream

225 g (8 oz) Greek yoghurt or crème fraiche

75 g (3 oz) demerara sugar

2 Put the fruit into individual heatproof dishes (or one large one). Sprinkle with lemon.

3 Whisk the double cream (see page 94) until it is thick, then mix with the yoghurt or crème fraiche.

Fresh fruit makes the perfect pudding. Even a big bunch of black grapes and some bright orange satsumas put on a serving plate can look very attractive, or if you've more time try one of these puddings. The first one is called 'Brulée' (burnt), because you 'burn' the sugar on top until it turns to caramel.

1 Get the fruit ready. If you're using the same as I have, then you need to peel the oranges and kiwi fruit, take the stones out of the apricots and wash the raspberries, grapes and apricots. Cut all the fruit into bite-sized pieces.

4 Spread the yoghurt and cream mixture over the fruit. Sprinkle the top with the demerara sugar.

5 🔥 Turn on the grill to high, and when it is hot put the fruit under it. Do be careful not to touch any part of the grill.

6 🔥 When the sugar has melted and is bubbling and looks as it it will soon start to burn, turn off the grill. Put on oven gloves and very carefully take the hot dishes out of the grill. Remember when you serve it that the sugar will stay very hot a long time, so watch your mouth!

VARIATIONS

1

Fresh Fruit Salad

Choose 3 or 4 kinds of fruit, different colours if possible. You could decide to have all tropical fruits: melon, kiwi and so on, or fruits like apple, oranges and strawberries. Prepare the salad as late as possible so it doesn't go brown and limp; not more than an hour or so before eating. Peel the fruit if necessary – but remember some, like green apples, are tastier with the peel left on. Take out any pips and cut carefully into bite-sized pieces. Pile the fruit into a pretty serving dish and squeeze the juice of ½ lemon all over it (this helps to stop it going brown). Or use a tall glass dish and put the fruit in layers to make a lovely centrepiece. Serve the fruit salad with cream or Greek yoghurt.

2

Jelly

Make up 2 packets of strawberry jelly as directed, but only add enough water to make 900 ml (1½ pints). Spoon a little into a 20-cm (8-in) square tin – just enough to cover the bottom. Chill until set. Cut 8 strawberries in half and press, cut side down, on to the jelly. Spoon a little jelly on top and chill until set (to stop the strawberries floating around when you cover them) then pour in enough jelly just to cover the strawberries, and chill until set. You should have almost ½ pint left. Add a little water (¼ pint) to the rest of the jelly, pour into a small mould and leave it to set. Turn out the large jelly on to a serving plate. Turn out the jelly square, cut it into sixteen squares and use them to decorate round the serving plate.

CRÊPES

Makes about 8   Medium easy

75 g (3 oz) plain flour

a pinch of salt

150 ml (5 fl oz) milk

1 egg

a little butter for frying

Crêpes is really just the smart word for pancakes. They should be a little thinner than the traditional English pancake, and you can fill them with all sorts of different things, both sweet and savoury. They are best of all eaten hot as soon as they are cooked, but if you want to make them ahead you can pile them on top of one another, wrap them in foil and heat them up later. This simple recipe for a basic pancake mix I learnt many years ago from a famous chef called Philip Harben.

1 Put the flour in a medium-sized bowl and mix in the salt.

2 Add a dash of water (about 1 tablespoon) to the measured milk.

3 Break the egg into the middle of the flour (break it into a cup first if you're worried about getting bits of shell in) and stir it with a whisk, letting bits of flour mix in as you do so. You can, of course, mix batter beautifully in a blender or processor but it's fine by hand.

4 While you keep whisking, add little by little the milk and water mixture. Don't worry about lumps, because they will go eventually. Carry on whisking until the batter, as it is now called, is lovely and smooth. Pour the batter into a jug. If you want to, you can now put the batter in the fridge for a few hours but it's not necessary.

5 When you're ready to cook the pancakes, take a heavy frying pan about 15 to 18 cm (6 to 7 in) across the bottom, and put it on a high heat. Let it get quite hot – about

half a minute – then put in a small piece of butter. Swirl the butter around as it melts, until the whole pan is covered with a very thin layer. You may find a brush is helpful. Leave the pan on the heat for a few more seconds until the butter is very hot, then turn down the heat to medium.

6 Pour a small amount of batter into the hot pan. It's impossible to tell you exactly how much – you can only learn by practice – but it's about 1 or 2 tablespoons. Quickly roll the pan around to spread the batter

evenly all over the pan; do it carefully as the pan will be very hot by now.

7 Let it cook for about 20 seconds then gently lift up the edge with a palette knife or fish slice: if it looks golden brown flip the pancake over (or toss if you like!) and cook for a few more seconds on the other side. Lift it carefully on to a plate and make the next

pancake. Strangely enough, I find the pancakes get easier to make as you go along – it's as if the frying pan gets into the swing of it somehow.

8 Either serve straight away with a squeeze of lemon and a sprinkling of sugar, or stack the pancakes on a plate, wrap in foil and use for one of these ideas.

FILLINGS

Sweet

Jam: Put a spoonful of strawberry or plum jam in the middle of each pancake, then roll it up, tucking in the ends as you go. Place them side by side on a baking tin or serving dish, sprinkle with caster sugar and put in a hot oven at 220°C (425°F), gas mark 7 for about 5 minutes until they are heated through. Serve with cream.

Chocolate: Spread each pancake with a spoonful of chocolate sauce (page 71) before heating. Serve with cream.

Savoury

Cheese and Ham: Make a thick white sauce by using recipe on page 62 but with half the milk. Add cheese, parsley, chopped cooked ham or chicken and put a spoonful in each pancake before brushing with melted butter and re-heating.

Frankfurter: Spread each pancake thinly with German mustard and add a frankfurter sausage before rolling up, sprinkling with grated cheese and heating.

FORTUNE COOKIES

Makes about 12   Medium easy

2 eggs

50 g (2 oz) sugar

a pinch of salt

50 g (2 oz) butter

50 g (2 oz) plain flour

a few drops of vanilla essence

I first had fortune cookies in a Chinese restaurant. Inside each little folded biscuit is a slip of paper with a message on it, and if you make your own you can have great fun thinking up what to write. Usually the fortunes are such things as 'beware of a tall stranger', but if you want to write 'you are a green fat toad' that's up to you . . .

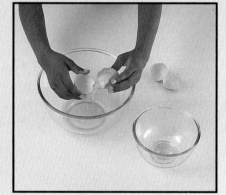

keeping the yolk in the shell (this is called separating the egg). If you drop any yolk in by mistake, fish it out with a teaspoon. You don't need the yolks for this recipe, so put them in an airtight pot or cover them with cling film and keep them in the fridge.

1 Turn on the oven to 180°C (350°F), gas mark 4. Write fortunes on 12 strips of paper, about 6 × 1 cm (2½ × ½ in) in size.

2 Carefully break each egg in half over a medium-sized bowl. Pass the egg from one half shell to the other, letting the white fall into the bowl, but

3 Stir the sugar into the egg whites and add the salt. Mix well. Melt the butter in a small saucepan or in the microwave and pour it into the eggs. Add the flour and vanilla and beat it all well together until smooth.

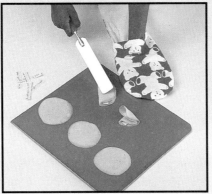

4 Drop the batter, 1 teaspoon at a time on to a greased baking sheet, making sure that the cookies are at least 5 cm (2 in) apart.

5 Put carefully into the oven for about 5 minutes, or until the edges are brown.

6 Wearing oven gloves, take the tray out of the oven. Being very careful of the hot tray, place a fortune in the middle of each cookie and fold over using a palette knife. Bend it again in the middle and hold for a few seconds until it keeps its shape. You have to work fast before the cookies get hard, so you may need help.

BASIC TECHNIQUES

PREPARING VEGETABLES

All vegetables need a really good wash before you do anything else. Even if they look clean they will almost certainly have been sprayed with pesticides at some point and these need to be cleaned off.

TO PREPARE GARLIC

Put the head of garlic on to the work surface. Give it a good hard tap with a mallet or rolling pin – you will find it splits neatly into cloves. Put one clove on the work surface and bash it with the mallet or pin. It will split, and the skin is then easy to take off with your fingers. Then you can either bash it a bit more until it's pulpy, or chop it carefully with a knife.

TO CHOP VEGETABLES

First peel if necessary. Cut the top and bottom off onions, then peel off the brown skin. Only peel carrots if they have tough skins. Cut the vegetable in half longways and cut slices across, not quite cutting through, so that it's still joined at one end. Then cut slices downwards one way, then across the other and you'll make neat squares. When chopping small vegetables, leave out the horizontal slices.

TO SLICE VEGETABLES

Hold the vegetable in your left hand (unless you're left-handed) with your fingers on top and bent. Hold the knife in your right hand and rest the side of the knife on your left hand fingers while you carefully move it up and down. Pull your fingers slowly back along the vegetable while you slice. If you find this difficult, do it a way that seems comfortable, but keep your fingers well away from the blade.

WHISKING

You can either use a fork, a whisk or an electric mixer. Move the fork or whisk in fast circles down to the bottom of the bowl and round up into the air before going round again. When whisking cream you must be very careful not to let it go too far or it will separate: keep stopping to check. It should be soft and thick.

BASIC RECIPES

SHORTCRUST PASTRY

100 g (4 oz) plain flour
25 g (1 oz) butter
25 g (1 oz) lard or white
cooking fat
a pinch of salt
about 2 tablespoons cold water

Put the flour and salt in a mixing bowl and cut the butter into it in small pieces. Pick up small handfuls of butter and flour and rub them between your fingertips and thumbs, thumbs upwards, letting the mixture fall back into the bowl. Keep on picking up and spreading the butter and flour over your fingers in this way until the mixture looks like breadcrumbs and there are no big lumps left. Add a little cold water bit by bit and stir it gently in until you can bring the mixture together in a ball with your hands. Gently – don't handle it too much – lift the pastry out of the bowl and wrap it in foil or cling film and put it in the fridge for 20 minutes before using it.

This quantity makes 100 g (4 oz) pastry since the amount of flour is always used to indicate the quantity needed. There is always half that amount of fat.

ICINGS

Butter Icing
Beat 50 g (2 oz) butter with a fork until it is soft, then bit by bit stir in 225 g (8 oz) sieved icing sugar. Add a little milk, water or fruit juice to make it thinner (you need it slightly thinner for spreading, thick enough to hold its shape for piping).

Chocolate Butter Icing
Add 50 g (2 oz) melted chocolate or 6 tablespoons cocoa powder mixed with a little boiling water to the butter icing.

Glacé Icing
Mix 225 g (8 oz) sieved icing sugar with about 2 tablespoons warm water or fruit juice. Add just enough liquid to make the icing coat the back of a spoon without it running off completely. Beat well.

Chocolate Glacé Icing
Add 4 to 6 tablespoons cocoa mixed with a little boiling water or 50 g (2 oz) melted chocolate to the glacé icing.

INDEX